A RICH BROTH

Memoirs of a Canadian Diplomat

DAVID

CHALMER

REECE

A RICH BROTH

Memoirs of a Canadian Diplomat

by

D A V I D   C H A L M E R   R E E C E

CARLETON UNIVERSITY PRESS
Ottawa, Canada
1993

CANADIAN CATALOGUING IN PUBLICATION DATA
Reece, David, 1926 –
   A rich broth: memoirs of a Canadian diplomat
   1. Reece, David, 1926–   . 2. Canada—Foreign relations. 3. Diplomatic
and consular service, Canadian—Biography. 4. Diplomats—Canada—
Biography. I. Title.
FC631.R44A3 1993   327.2'092   C93-090268-8   F1034.3.R44A3 1993
ISBN 0-88629-204-2 (casebound) — ISBN 0-88629-205-0 (paperback)

Distributed by: Oxford University Press Canada
               70 Wynford Drive
               Don Mills, Ontario
               Canada M3C 1J9
               (416) 441-2941

Cover and interior design by Colton Temple Design.

Acknowledgements
   Carleton University Press gratefully acknowledges the support extend-
ed to its publishing programme by the Canada Council and the Ontario Arts
Council.
   The Press would also like to thank the Department of Communications,
Government of Canada, and the Government of Ontario through the
Ministry of Culture, Tourism and Recreation, for their assistance.

ACKNOWLEDGEMENTS

To Nina, who lived and edited it with élan, and to our children for their cheerful survival of such mobility. They made it more fun than stress. Our thanks to Canadian, diplomatic and foreign colleagues who shared the life and work. We much regret that the diplomatic merry-go-round makes it so hard to sustain friendships.

We are grateful to the Director of Carleton University Press, Michael Gnarowski, and the staff who, under the editorship of Anne Winship, made many improvements in this text.

I remember with gratitude two excellent teachers at Ravenscourt school in Winnipeg, Percy Wykes and Ogden Turner. They taught history and literature with lasting benefit to their students.

TABLE OF CONTENTS

PREFACE

Diplomatic memoirs are in abundance. So why write more? My excuse is that this book is based on experience wider than most. In thirty-eight years with External Affairs I had ten postings on five continents. I also had five periods in Ottawa and one in Quebec City, plus two slices of temporary duty abroad. In five out of the ten postings I was ambassador or high commissioner (the title for Commonwealth envoys in Commonwealth countries).

In describing this moveable feast, I draw on substantive diplomatic fare but also try to illustrate what Canadian diplomats actually do and how my wife, family, and I coped with our curious lives of outward mobility. These memoirs may also entertain a little since they touch on the quaint, comic, and bizarre encounters which seem more common abroad than at home.

Two of my postings were to multilateral delegations seeking agreement in international committees and conferences. My job as minister and deputy representative in our United Nations delegation in New York entailed minor achievements but also, in my experience, built-in frustrations. My four years as ambassador and head of delegation to the East-West arms control negotiations in Vienna did not see the achievement of a balanced force reductions treaty, but an agreement was reached in a successor forum.

And the Vienna talks were in themselves a useful injection of détente.

As I circulated among bilateral posts, there were meetings, occasions, and dealings with a wide range of leaders including Prime Minister Indira Gandhi of India, President Kaunda of Zambia, Prime Minister Seaga of Jamaica, and various other third world heads of government; Canadian Prime Ministers Diefenbaker, Pearson, Trudeau, and Mulroney; and a rich broth of domestic and foreign cabinet ministers, provincial satraps, state governors, tribal chiefs, senior officials, development experts, bankers, journalists, cultural stars, local characters, and ordinary people. From these diplomatic experiences I sketch some tentative conclusions.

My father began this book — in a sense. I suggested he write an account of his vivid life. But it was too late. He was too ill to tackle it. So I wrote my own version of his Welsh sparkle and our warm family life in Winnipeg fifty and sixty years ago. And then I kept on going. In so doing I relied on a tenacious memory aided by diaries and letters.

CHAPTER ONE

Family

MY FATHER, Rupert Reece, was a volatile Welshman. His temperament was a toboggan slide steepened by gout in his later years. He was one of four brothers raised by a tough and worldly widower who was an Anglican vicar in North Wales. According to family legend, Grandfather once accompanied a wealthy local widow on a world cruise in the role of private chaplain. The night they sailed, his parishioners shook the church with a heartfelt rendition of "For Those In Peril on the Sea." His habit of battling with his church superiors confined his ceiling to the modest role of canon of the smallest cathedral in Britain. The canon's own father was held by family lore to have been a gentleman farmer in South Wales; research into the records by a barrister cousin of mine has unearthed his real métier: he was a barber in Birmingham.

After some years in a rugged public school in Lancashire, my father was given the choice of studying theology at Oxford or entering commerce. He instantly chose the latter and soon found himself on the way to Winnipeg in 1911, representing a Liverpool firm of grain merchants. On the dockside his father gave him five pounds — even then not a gold mine — and said, "Be careful who your friends are, my boy." The reply was swift — "I'll have to be goddamn careful with only five quid in my pocket!"

Despite his own thrifty parent, I am not sure my father was very keen on business — or very good at it. For example, after three or four years of

marriage, he took my mother on a luxurious holiday near Banff. As the sun
set over the Rockies on the last day, he mentioned that the hotel bill for
their stay would complete his demolition of her substantial dowry. The rest
had been lost in unwise trading in wheat futures on the Grain Exchange.

Certainly my father did not spend all his time on the export of grain. His
puckish and sometimes ribald sense of humour added spice to his chair-
manship of many local organizations. He was a polymath of worthy causes including a wide spectrum of voluntary war work in the 1940s. He also
represented the Grain Exchange on a wartime government advisory committee representative of farmers, grain pools, and similar bodies. Characteristically, his favourite colleague on this committee was a colourful
prairie wheat pool leader, Jack Weston, who hotly opposed the free market system so passionately favoured by the Grain Exchange. The only time
I ever heard my father say "sir" was when the relevant cabinet minister
phoned to appoint him to the Committee. His acceptance was a wartime
concession to the Liberals since he was a staunch Tory.

As a member of the Grain Exchange Council for many years and its president for a time, both elected offices, my father was popular with rumbus-
tious colleagues in that rather uproarious institution. He was proud of the
salute he received from one of them: "Rupe, you're the best friend the
drunks ever had!" He described another as "blowing apart" rather than
simply dying of a stroke. At the subsequent funeral a fellow drinker of
Scottish origin was seen tucking a bottle of whisky into the hand of the
departed in his open coffin — a pharaonic gesture for the long journey.
But it was only a "mickey" — twelve ounces. A bonny thought but not
extravagant.

When my father arrived in Winnipeg the Exchange was at its rollicking
height of boom and bust before World War I. Although the boom was predominant, Stony Mountain Penitentiary welcomed members who had cut
it too fine in trading on margin. Others allegedly disappeared on holiday
to Florida — or anywhere — while actually serving a short prison term for
impaired driving. A more harmless drunk used to arrive on our doorstep
every January 1 preceded by a tipsy piper bagging in the New Year.

Two brothers who were grain brokers were among my father's closest
friends in his early years in Winnipeg. All three were bachelors and all

drank heartily. On one occasion my father was taking tea with the dragon mother of these two when she pointed out with pride that they never touched a drop of liquor. My father, haggard with a giant hangover acquired in their company a few hours earlier, remained shaken and silent.

My father's span of thirty-five years in Winnipeg was broken by four and a half years of service in World War I. He started in the ranks in a Canadian regiment but switched to a Welsh unit after Canon Reece used some genteel pull. In Bedford, England, where he was an instructor in grenade warfare, he attracted his future mother-in-law's attention. "Who is that foulmouthed fellow who is always cursing his troops?" she asked. Mother refrained from saying that he was her future husband. But she married in 1917. Her father was not there to hand her over. He was playing happy hooky from the family tool factory in Sheffield commanding the depot of a British reserve unit in Poona, India. It was a lucky unlucky war for this grandfather since enteric fever caught in India gave him a welcome reason to retire with honour at fifty-three and revel in his hobbies of history, archaeology, and anthropology. With a lawyer son-in-law, he published a two-volume work entitled *Law in the Light of History*.

The newly-married Rupert Reece did not reach Winnipeg until 1919. He was stuck on garrison duty in Germany after the war. As battalion education officer, he was ordered to find out which vocational courses his troops wanted to take — a device aimed more at saving the local town maidens than at spreading education among the military. By remarkable coincidence, his entire unit opted for beekeeping. This little gem of my father's whimsy was no doubt the reason why the final rating on him by his commanding officer, which I found with delight in a trunk years later, was a diplomatic masterpiece of faint praise and barely concealed malice. My father must have been one of the few young infantry officers who saw service in France during World War I and remained a lieutenant for the entire period after his routine promotion from second lieutenant. Hassling superiors was an unprofitable family trait.

In Winnipeg his zestful breadth of voluntary activity was augmented by a heavy social life even by local standards. But he still gave much warmth and fun to his family. His Christmas charades were a vivid dream of childhood. The cast included two Welsh friends: a genial cherub from the Welsh

Chapel, the Rev. Gronger Stephens, and a Calgary lawyer from Cardiff whom my father had helped lure into a Winnipeg grain company. L.W. ("Brock") Brockington later became famous as an orator endowed with the Welsh *hwyl*,* wartime speech writer for Mackenzie King and chairman of the CBC. But I always think of his portrait of a Welsh washerwoman played with accented hilarity opposite my father in matching bonnet. Another Christmas, my father used a roll of toilet paper to represent the *Winnipeg Free Press* before its unamused editor.

An occasional source of delight to his small sons was his "Wild Man of Borneo" act. He ran along the upstairs corridor in a state of undress. His real Welsh wild man origins were not forgotten in Winnipeg. He played a leading role in the St. David's Society and seemed to be one of the few from Wales who were well-heeled or even employed in the Depression of the '30s. I recall my distress at a very down-at-heel man who came to our front door in the mid-'30s and said in a ripe Welsh accent, "I know your father, lad. I'm very hungry. Can you give me a sandwich?" I gave him some of my own crude cut. Because we were Anglicans of professional heritage, we did not attend the very modest basement chapel of the largely Methodist Welsh community, but we turned up for Christmas carols. In that low-ceilinged room the soaring strong Welsh voices seemed to be bulging the walls. Although my father was a rarity, an unmusical son of Wales, he could not escape his national heritage entirely. When the executive committee of the St. David's Society paid a farewell call on him in the hotel just before our family departure from Winnipeg in 1946, Mfanwy Evans, a lovely and locally renowned singer, accompanied them. She sang "Mae hen wlad fy Nhadau" (Land of my fathers) with feeling and force which more than filled our hotel suite. Then all present burst into tears. The words of that song and a few other tag lines were unfortunately all that my father inherited of the lovely Welsh language from his father who was bilingual and preached in both. (My own family is very aware of the Reece origins. When we spent a few days in Wales in 1984 we were enchanted to find a concert party performing in Welsh on the beach front in Aberystwyth. We shamelessly eavesdropped on conversations around that university and seaside town. There seemed to be more Welsh spoken by middle class families —

* hwyl = "an emotional quality which inspires and sustains impassioned eloquence."

perhaps a sign of the conscious effort being made by academics, intellectuals, and politicians to preserve Welsh culture and language. I hope they succeed but it is a vertical climb.)

My father's zigzag emotional tract was fully exerted when I came home to announce that I had just switched from the university reserve to active service in the Navy in May 1944. He literally kicked my butt. He thought one son killed in the war was enough. The next day, however, he rented a car for me to use for my last few days of civilian life. (My brother had driven the final guts out of our wheezy Ford V8 on the road between Portage and Winnipeg in 1941 during his air-training days, a year before his death.)

My father would have been happy to stay in the carriage age. He was dangerously inept in mechanics. He clung to an ice box as long as they would deliver blocks of ice to the door. Our rather speedy cars (one at a time) were grossly neglected and driven with celerity. On one occasion after a party the car came at speed to a well sign-posted barrier diverting traffic from a hole in the road under repair. Too late to stop. My father obeyed the military maxim that, when your flanks are crumbling, charge! The car hurdled the deep but narrow crevasse leaving the wooden barrier in disarray.

Somehow there was never a serious accident, perhaps because my father preferred to walk to work, gout permitting, or take a taxi. He claimed he had never travelled on public transport in Winnipeg. This did not jibe, however, with a favourite anecdote about a tragedy he had witnessed. A shabby old man was travelling on a street car in Winnipeg on Christmas Eve, happily clutching a forty ounce bottle of gin. The car swayed and lurched and the bottle smashed on the floor. The old man muttered "Christmas come ... and gone."

My father had kindred friends across Canada as a result of his service on national committees of the grain trade and voluntary organizations. One boisterous friend became a lieutenant governor. He dropped in to see my father once at our hotel when we were paying a brief visit to his province. A long afternoon wore on punctuated by His Excellency's attempts to escape from my father's flowing hospitality. It became clear after a while that he did not really want to escape, although he made regular pious references to the need to drive off and "visit my people," and sign a bill

*Brother Michael and David with father Rupert Reece in front of
family home in Winnipeg, 1941.*

into law at the legislature. Finally he summoned his driver and with the
driver and me holding him up at each side, we made weaving progress
through the lobby to his car at the door. Disaster. The local bishop hove in
sight. But the instincts of the lieutenant governor, who was a World War I
veteran, were in better shape than his legs. "Hello, Padre," he shouted
cheerfully as he was helped past.

His childlike gusto for organizing elaborate outings and happenings
endeared my father to his two children and to their friends, who must have
found their own fathers a shade pallid. We children of this high-coloured
parent were, of course, proud of his wide appeal to our contempories. He
had in effect an extended family audience for his eccentricities and jokes.
But this outer circle of entertainees got the smooth side only. They missed
the rough ripples of his gout attacks which grew worse with the years and
were a general family disaster. But even in the pain of a swollen elbow or
knee he could sometimes enjoy a chuckle. "Touch of the old trouble, sir?"
said a taxi driver, one veteran to another, as my father hobbled into the cab.
There was no demur. Another source of envy for my friends was a growing flow, as we grew older, of Rabelaisian jokes from the Grain Exchange,
presumably hatched and polished by grain brokers between trading sessions. These crude gems were the life blood of school recess.

Whether or not attacked by gout or brimming with spirits from the liquor store, my father had a bi-polar temperament, and the up-pole was the stronger. When a child knocked over a glass during a meal, he might celebrate, or reprove, by sweeping glasses, plates, and utensils to the floor from a wide circle at his end of the table. In imitating with ardour an acquaintance with a shaky hand, he also destroyed fragile utensils with esprit. We would not have traded him. Few small boys would have.

My mother was a reserved woman who gave her children warmth and love without display. She nursed me with strength and patience through years of serious illness in lower childhood. She was quietly devastated by my brother's death, my father less quietly. She was firmly effective in facing my father's abundant ebullience but she was a neo-Victorian wife in mode and temperament. She had a passion for the cleanly and she once fired a cook she found gargling in the sink. She had many friends in Winnipeg's more affluent circles and what passed for Manitoba's aristocracy. This milieu my parents enjoyed and were accepted in, through admiration for their "correct" English accent rather than excess of cash. We lived in a slightly decaying old suburb inhabited by scions of two or three of Canada's few titled families plus local political and commercial nabobs. Three of these houses were pulled down in decrepitude when I was quite young and all have gone now, including our own more humble but large frame house.

My mother liked Winnipeggers, even some of the rowdies, but she never lost her heart to the place. From verdant English woods she arrived in her new home on the flat prairie dotted with five-foot high trees. The General Strike of 1919 was in full spate. Kind friends had put an unplucked and ungutted chicken in the ice box. My gentle English mother brought up by a governess and a Brussels finishing school could not pluck, much less eviscerate, a fowl. But she learned to handle the prairie and my father. According to family legend, my mother and I almost perished of cold the night I was born in our first small house on the outer edge of the city on February 14, 1926. Celebrating, my father let the furnace go out. If true, I suspect he got quiet hell for it in the morning, Valentine's Day or not.

My brother Michael, three and a half years older than I, was a joyous gadgeteer with strong social gifts. His room was alive with models, posters,

Meccano mobiles, and purloined signs including a flashing neon adver-
tisement for a soft drink. Scholarship was not his love. His marks were
sometimes in the sixties. I did not look forward to the arrival of the report
cards from school. My father's verbal chastisement of big brother was translated into light corporal punishment for bright little brother with the high
marks. Science and applied commerce were Michael's preferences. He and
a partner had a successful juvenile photography firm. The results and prof-
its were good. Michael (widely known as "Ike") was handsome, genial, and
outgoing. He had a wide range of friends, many of them outside the school
where he spent ten years — half of his meagre span. He had ample success
with the opposite sex.

His Hurricane fighter was seen confronting two German Messer-
schmidts before he crash-landed in Egypt on August 1, 1942. This was during the lowest point of Allied fortunes against Rommel. In his last ten days
of life in the military hospital in Alexandria, Michael showed that despite
his burns and wounds he did not give up easily, neither his life nor his sense
of fun and irreverence. In a book of wartime reminiscence, one of his nurses, Helen Vlasto (now Long), devotes two pages to him as a favourite
patient. She wrote, "For the few days that he lived he kept us all cheered
up with his teasing and spirited back-chat, and the charm and courage that
radiated from his corner ... he would call across to a chap in a bed opposite to 'drop something on the floor' in order that he could tease the next
nurse to pass that way to bend and pick it up, and so rouse the others
to wolf whistles."* He died on August 10, aged barely 20. His school magazine noted that he left behind him a "trail of merry memories." A very
short trail.

---

* Helen Long, *Change Into Uniform*, Terence Dalton Ltd, 1978.

CHAPTER TWO

School and University
(1933-46)

IN THE BEGINNING I hated school. I attended the first three grades of Grosvenor Public School in Winnipeg although still clawed by asthma which had delayed my school start. I was shy and unwarlike, natural fodder for bullies, and was incapable of acquiring friends and protectors. The only exception was a blundering but kind boy from my neighbourhood, Tom Riley, who offered to lend me his unsheathed pen as a weapon. I declined, fearing to unleash answering fists.

My parents must have detected my quiet misery at Grosvenor and switched me to a small private boys' school, Ravenscourt, where my brother was in cheerful attendance. I jumped two grades, enjoyed the organized fun and games, and quickly found friends in small classes, friends I retain. Well behind in French, I authored a classic schoolboy howler in translating *merci beaucoup* as "Mercy, what a lot."

I had eight happy years at Ravenscourt, 1935-43. I became school captain (head boy) in the last year. My father was chairman of the Board of Governors but my selection as captain had less to do with this, I submit, than with the slim competition from my peers. My marks were good to very good, but I came under severe challenge in the upper years from a scientifically-bent scholar who later became a professor of astrophysics at Harvard. My scholarship was temporarily impaired by a friend's BB pellet which skimmed accidentally across my eye en route to a gopher during summer holidays on a farm. Although generally good at games, my early invalid years and an innate clumsiness kept me off the hockey team, to the benefit of my basketball. I am ashamed to admit that I inserted, for the first time in the school magazine, a set of basketball statistics. These displayed me on the top rung, by curious coincidence. I was by no means the best player but was fed by unselfish team mates. I managed to lumber in first in the mile and the half-mile races in my last year, aided by the heavy smoking of my chief rival. This also enabled me to beat him in the annual boxing tourney, a compulsory orgy of unskilled youths hurting each other.

A more piquant triumph was on the stage, in a laborious production of "Toad of Toad Hall," by A.A. Milne. Another boy, cast in the role of Toad, was soon relegated to washerwoman because he could not memorize the lines of this wordy play. My own dramatic skills were limited but, boy, could I memorize! In the event, this four-hour marathon "was, you might say, satisfactory," but the glue fastening my puff-cheeked frog makeup attacked me with asthma that night. My virulent allergy to fish even extended to the glue made then of fish bones. My father, who had complained cheerfully about the length and aridity of the evening (i.e., the time between drinks), nonetheless urged me to act again on the second and last night. It was a family joke that from my bedridden wheezing carcass that morning came a heroic gasp, "The show must go on!" So it did and my enforced economy of breath made the second Toad better than the first.

Thereafter the theatre saw my talents seldom except in skits of my own would-be humorous make. "The Saga of Siegfried Snerd," written in collaboration with a student Wagnerian, won top prize at a Manitoba University contest thanks to the Wagnerian's "Death of Wotan". This was a strangulated and prolonged bout of histrionics, disrupted by a nubile coed who ran across the stage pursued by the only male in the Interior Decoration Faculty. At Cambridge I was recruited for the college revue because of my accent and to impress my then light-of-love. She was not impressed and disliked my accent. In my first months in Ottawa, I wrote a skit for a departmental Christmas party which is said to have displeased the then Minister of External Affairs, Lester B. Pearson, by implying that he was pushed around by his chief female assistant and by underlining the paucity of his postings abroad when in the Foreign Service. Despite this,

James ("Si") Taylor, who played Pearson, rose to the top rank in the service. Quality will out on the boards and in the board room.

Charades have since been my only stage, and my family and house guests my only audience. My efforts reek of heavy ham and, according to my children, a thick slice of cheating. The former reached impossible heights one night when I acted out solo *Vile Bodies* and then *Othello* as integral entities. It was a cacophony of writhing, mugging, and frenzy never achieved again.

School Teachers

No scholastic chapter is complete without a love/hate portrait of eccentric masters. At Ravenscourt we had a ripe collection, including the Latin teacher who could hit errant pupils at ten yards with a stinging piece of chalk. He was popular nonetheless because of his habit of slinging his books on the floor and, feet on desk, rambling the hour away with tales of rural Manitoba and the "hobo jungles" he had frequented. A stern science master proclaimed the vegetarian habits of catfish. By joyous chance, we were able to produce in class the next day a catfish with a smaller fish clamped in its jaws, garnered from the adjacent confluence of school sewer and the Red River. The teacher was speechless. His successor had a cheery chipmunk mien but compelling means. He set many an "or else" test ... get 100% or the strap. Marks were high in his class. A teacher of French, a charming Swiss, earned grumbles from my father for writing a novel during his tenure. He was apparently expected to spend all his waking hours on pedagogy. Charm did not save him from little-boy torture when Christopher Young, appropriately a future journalist of distinction, emptied a fountain pen of ink into his upturned mouth. "I vill not be a vitness to dese tings!" cried the cultivated Swiss as he fled from the room. Another teacher short on discipline was amazed when half his class walked through the door after being in their places a minute before. They had hopped out the window when his back was turned. Another distraught teacher caused mass strapping of our class by displaying a wide open fly which led to loud hilarity and the headmaster's disapproval.

The school bursar, or administrator, a venerable worthy nicknamed "Creeping Jesus" by one of the roughneck boarders from the Lakehead, was an inevitable target. Despite his appearance of benevolent sleepiness, he did a good job in tough wartime conditions which had led to sharply reduced enrollment. The headmaster, who was capable and exigent, delighted in the Latin grace at lunch time. We all had to stand in reverent silence during this performance then scramble down on our benches and grab for the bread piled high on plates in the middle of the table. A boy tried to jump the gun and was forked in the hand. The headmaster was not entertained.

As a schoolboy I spent most summer holidays on flat prairie farms. My father's grain trade disposed him to this solution. My parents were not lake or cottage enthusiasts. Schooldays ended, the summer of 1943 looked like more fun. With some Ravenscourt friends, I found a job in a shipyard in Vancouver. Unhappily, it was just as dreary as the farm and the rooms in the workers' hostel were less appetizing. We worked six days a week as electricians' assistants, screwing in light bulbs and stringing up wires in the boiler room of a ship. Naturally, it was the most glorious summer of all time in British Columbia memory; bright, clear, and sunny every day. Our vigorous efforts to get on the night shift failed. We spent our sabbath ration of daylight on the beach or at the race track.

The six-day week was caused by submarine warfare eating into allied shipping. The yards were making and repairing merchant and naval ships badly needed in the Atlantic and Pacific. I worked in the bowels of an armed merchant cruiser which was being converted into a tank-landing mother ship eventually used in the invasion of southern France in 1944. My patriotic zeal was, however, dulled by the grubby banality of the work. The electrician I helped, a tedious but good-natured and skillful man, essayed a little joke about all summer workers being conscripted into labour in the yards for the duration of the war. I almost clubbed him with rage and relief when he confessed his gag. It was dispiriting to see and literally run across nests of sleeping and card-playing idlers in quiet pockets of the ship. In contrast were some energetic and entertaining left-wing exhorters. My favourite was "Pete the Russian," who did not seem aware of Stalinist evils and was the soul of geniality in his broken English. The naval personnel, especially the petty officers, were often disagreeable to us.

Considering this insipid summer, it is surprising that I eventually joined the Navy. I did so largely because my friends did, and because I was understandably allergic to the R.C.A.F. But before my short military career got

Ravenscourt graduates between classes at the University of Manitoba, 1943. David on the left.

going, I did my first year (1943-44) at the University of Manitoba. Returning after war service, I completed another year at the University of Manitoba before moving to England with my parents who were leaving Winnipeg after thirty-five years to return to work and live in London.

My two years at the University of Manitoba, split by war service, left me one year short of a degree. My general arts course was too broad to be of much use. It included rather feeble attempts at philosophy and psychology. But we did have stimulating English professors as well as a magisterial history don (a title he would have liked), Noel Fieldhouse, whose electrifying lectures on the French Revolution at 8:00 A.M. on frigid prairie winter days amidst singing radiators are impossible to forget. It was he who first mentioned a foreign service career to us in class. More than twenty years later I met him again when he was Vice-Principal of McGill University receiving a visit from the Prime Minister of India, Lal Bahadur Shastri, whom I was accompanying. I shook him so enthusiastically by the hand then that he spilled his sherry on his waistcoat. He did not remember me but I subsequently used one of his dictums in arms control talks in Vienna.

My second, post-war year at Manitoba was frolic and drinking up the war service gratuity. We almost killed ourselves on the rugby field in fierce, unskilled fraternity games. A few of these fraternity warriors also played in a much tougher league, as second stringers for the Winnipeg Blue Bombers, the professional team which competed for the Grey Cup. I played on the scrimmage line against one of these part-time pros during a very long afternoon spent largely on my back.

I did somewhat better on my feet as an all-star debater, not a role I had expected. It was thrust upon me by the convenor of extramural debates, a sardonic senior. He chose me to accompany him in a debate against the University of Minnesota, but mainly to do the basic research for our topic, "Should there be Free Trade between Canada and the United States?" An evergreen. My only experience was in inter-faculty debate plus holding down, silently, a cabinet portfolio in the student mock parliament. A letter appeared in the student press accusing us of nepotism.

With this cloud at our back, we arrived by train in Minneapolis, a great metropolis to us, even though we considered Winnipeg the Chicago of Canada. We goggled at well-stocked liquor stores where permits to purchase were not needed. We bought like kids in candy. This had congenial effects on our social life!

The debate was a winner. First we had an early and uninspired supper with our opponents, both theology students. They bulged with sincerity. Noting also signs of orthodox inflexibility, we were encouraged. By the restrictive formula of North American debating, we each had ten minutes for opening statements and then three minutes for rebuttal. Unbridled eloquence was curbed, perhaps just as well since our opponents had a square-jawed pulpit glibness. In a gallant attempt at humour, I began with a reference to personally promoting a northward trade movement in whisky, Lucky Strike cigarettes, and nylon stockings, then in short supply in Canada. The issue seemed in balance after the openers but the equilibrium tipped swiftly in the rebuttals. The theologians were wooden while our liberal training produced quips and cuts galore. The judges were unanimous. Their chief came to congratulate us afterwards. He was a sparkling, ebullient man, the Mayor of Minneapolis, Hubert Humphrey, later senator, vice-president, and almost president. Buoyed by his charm and good judgement, we shed our deflated foes and set off into the good life of the Minneapolis night.

CHAPTER THREE

Navy
(1944-45)

THE FIRST ASSIGNMENT of my 17 months of war service took place thousands of miles from the sea. At Shepley Island in the Saskatchewan River just south of Saskatoon, I passed the summer of 1944 as an instructor of sea cadets.

I was accompanied by two friends who were also college students and less than nineteen and thus too young to prepare for selection as probationary sub-lieutenants. On the island we were pitched in with a crew of tough stokers. They too had never seen a ship but one or two of them had seen the inside of a coal mine. None could have been accused of having a genteel or affluent background. They did the camp maintenance and dirty work while we taught sea cadets knots and signals and how to pull an oar.

After a tense period of suspicion, the two solitudes in one tent settled down together. Under the influence of a rugged miner from Alberta, the stokers decided we were harmless although very wet. We grew fond of one miner who had an admirable morality which said, in effect, that to get drunk, fornicate, and brawl was fine but you must on no account fail to be honest in every way. We boys liked to think that our weekly trips to town with our pals the stokers caused the locals to "grow gray with fear and tremble and despoil themselves" (as Shelley put it) at the approach of the Shepley Island Gang.

*David (far right) and Chris Young (far left) at the Sea Cadet camp on
Shepley Island, 1944.*

Before beginning my officer's training in Halifax in May 1945, I was
attached as a supernumerary deck officer to two training ships in a row for
a few weeks each. The first was a "four-stacker," an ex-U.S. Navy destroy-
er with four funnels. Its captain was amazed to see my apprentice performance in "conning" the ship, that is, directing it from the bridge. The exercise was to throw a large waterproof barrel over the side while the ship was
going at a good clip. By giving orders to the helmsman, the neophyte officer was supposed to take the ship in a wide circle to pick up the barrel.
Mine disappeared forever.

I was transferred to H.M.C.S. *Collingwood*, a "one-lung" corvette (one
boiler out of action) in April 1945. At this final stage of the naval war the
Germans were making a dying effort to choke Allied supplies by using a
large number of submarines equipped with snorkel gear which enabled
them to stay under water for long periods far from their bases. These subs
could therefore cruise easily near the North American coastline and in the
Gulf of St. Lawrence. (A former U-boat officer told me ten years later that
they were in fact well up the St. Lawrence when the war ended. The crew

took a vote to decide whether to surrender in Canada or in the United States or to try to make it all the way to potential freedom in South America. The vote was almost unanimous for the U.S.A. where POW camps were thought to be more comfy than in bleak, cold Canada.) Two Canadian naval ships were sunk by subs near Halifax, in late 1944 and April 1945. Under these circumstances even a "one lunger" was pressed into convoy duty. Our ship, the *Collingwood*, escorted three freighters down the coast from New Brunswick to Portland, Maine, a few hundred miles but in the process we lost one of them, not to subs but to rocks and fog in American waters. While waiting for the U.S. Coast Guard to take over the wounded vessel, the captain of our ship was called from the bridge and left me alone in charge, quaking with memories of the lost barrel. He ordered me to circle a buoy because ships cannot just stand still. "Whatever you do, don't lose sight of it!" This time, in reverse geometry to the barrel disaster, I hung in there for a circle or two, my first and last time in lonely command at sea.

On our way back from Portland with three or four ships in convoy, we ran out of war. On the day before the official V-E Day, we were ordered to light ship (light up) and stow our weapons. Since the crew of our ship included green trainees, and our main weapon was a "squid" apparatus which threw small missiles designed to explode on contact, I was a shade anxious, especially as we were now highly visible. I wondered whether the German navy had been as prompt with its orders. Needless to say, we arrived unscathed in Saint John in time for the official V-E Day.

We had been ordered to refuel there and then proceed immediately to our base in Cornwallis. During our stay half the town of Saint John came down to the docks to celebrate, including some friendly prostitutes. This was my real moment of danger. I was officer of the day in charge of discipline and decorum. "No, fellows, you can't go ashore ... Captain's orders," all in my teenage voice. My popularity sank even lower when we anchored at Cornwallis; by then it was too late to go ashore and join the lusty celebrations there. These remained under control, in contrast to the Halifax riots.

My role as Scrooge on V-E Day had a sequel. When attending a hockey game in Winnipeg about six months later, dressed appropriately in Joe College outfit, I saw two sniggering men looking at me in derisive fashion,

one pointing at me. They were sailors from the *Collingwood* doubtlessly
sneering, "Look at that young jerk who used to pretend he was an officer
on our ship."

CHAPTER FOUR

Cambridge
(1946-49)

BECAUSE OF PAST family affiliations and my parents' return to England in 1946, I chose Cambridge as my next step in academia. I had a first drudging year of history under an unsuitable supervisor of studies who was acidly disparaging. He described more than one essay, heavy with prairie effort, as "such a wash of words." I slugged hard at my books to near melancholia; everything looked brown. Although I got respectable results in the history exams, I decided that my idea of becoming a scholar was unrealistic. As an American friend put it, I lacked "ass-power." So I switched to law.

Unfortunately, I loathed the law despite good tutors and an international law professor, Hersch Lauterpacht, whose lectures conjured up the ancient universities of Mittel-Europa. He was a splendid figure and an ace in the field. But the rest was sawdust. It is, I suppose, character-building to plough through a degree course in a field for which you have no appetite, but it is bloody boring.

To help justify the switch, also born of "now-or-never" Canadian government veterans' grant requirements, I told myself that I should become a politician. Use the law as a vehicle, etc. Joining the Cambridge Union was the obvious but formidable next move. The Union, the university's debating society and student parliament, unofficially divided along party political lines, was the venerable cradle of statesmen. Equipped with a "capitalist" Canadian accent oddly married to left-of-centre views recently acquired, I did surprisingly well although my forensic ability and speed of thought were not remarkable. I was much aided by a friend in my college, Percy Cradock, a brilliant scholar from Durham, who eventually capped a shining diplomatic career by appointment as senior advisor to No. 10 Downing Street. Mrs. Thatcher had been impressed by his part in the negotiations over Hong Kong when he was ambassador to China.

Under Percy's wing I soon won Labour Club endorsement for Cambridge Union Committee membership to which I was elected three times consecutively over the prostrate bodies of future Tory cabinet ministers and the like. One I did not beat was an urbane and talented amuser called Norman St. John Stevas, who later served in Thatcher's cabinet and is now in the House of Lords. He beat me by thirty votes for secretary of the Union and by only three votes for vice-president. My elections to the Union Committee, which had a considerable Conservative majority at the time, were partly due to assiduous Labour canvassers and the floating vote. Canvassing was illegal but our supporters did it in Hindi, Malay, Urdu, Malayalam, Singalese, Chinese, etc. Detection was thus difficult.

I also picked up support by writing reviews of debates and general articles for the student newspaper. One such, co-authored by Cradock, was entitled "Night Climbers of Cambridge." We sought the views of the president of the Mountain Climbing Society of Cambridge. Surely the techniques involved in traversing a crevasse in the Himalayas must be akin to leaping dangerously over an ancient college alleyway on the way up to planting a chamber pot atop King's College Chapel? This odious comparison was denied with acrimony by the mountaineer.

Politics as an alternative career ended for me one night when I took part, at fatally short notice, in a debate of censure on the President of the Union. I was savaged by St. John Stevas and a waspish Ceylonese from the Labour Club who crossed the floor to shred my case. Shattered by these attacks and bailed out by a Labour colleague, Bill Wedderburn, who later became a Life peer, I looked in the mirror of the Union Committee room and said to myself, "You'll never make a politician." And I have never seriously thought to be one since. A tutor, thinking quite wrongly that I had tricked him in a matter of some importance, asked me, "What on earth are you going to do for a living?" I said diplomacy might be the way. He approved because he thought I had the "right combination of candour and deceit."

Apart from union activities and presiding over the St. John's College Debating Society, and the Canada Club, which alternated distinguished speakers with beer swilling, my Cambridge career was ho-hum. My law results were good but fell short of brilliant. Scattered gleams of fun spun off the incandescent social life of a sparkling English lad who shared my set of college rooms for two years. On one occasion five other students gathered in our neighbour's room to decide what to do about a young woman they had all been sleeping with (not me). Sent home from the local school of nursing for pinching a ten shilling note, she had got off the train at a nearby station and had come back looking for succour from her old college pals. After a brief parley, it was unanimously decided to have nothing further to do with her after this shocking theft. An intriguing look at British student morality.

I owed to my roommate a unique outburst in a dank winter. I joined him as a stuntman at the annual humour magazine ball. This mainly consisted of heaving food and crockery in all directions from the middle of the ballroom. Thus stimulated, I encountered the chief of university discipline, the Senior Proctor, a faculty member burdened with the task of laying hands on miscreant undergraduates. He was accompanied by "bulldogs," hefty college porters. He was rightly feared since he could recommend expulsion if university rules were too severely fractured. Undeterred and heavily disguised in my stuntman garb, I heaved with accuracy a small cabbage in my possession and struck the Proctor a glancing blow on the head. Although I had engulfed pints and quarts of Cambridge beer, I had enough moxie left to disappear at full throttle. I later boasted of this rash crime at an inter-college debate where the Senior Proctor himself was one of the other speakers. He took this to be a privileged occasion and sportingly noted that he had thrown the cabbage back but had missed me.

My lunches in the college hall (i.e., dining room) were deep in cabbages. Fish was a staple and meat very short in post-war austerity Britain. I was still very allergic to fish and would ask for something else. "Oh, vegetarian, sir," was the invariable response. We had several Asian students of that habit. I joined them with a deep sigh. Asia, however, helped out after lunch. There was an Indian restaurant nearby which contrived somehow to make tasty jam omelets out of dried eggs in the absence of tightly rationed or non-existent real eggs. Goodness knows where the jam came from in the land of rationing. The end product was ambrosia after college cooked vegetables.

Cambridge recreations were lustier than cabbages and omelets. An encounter with a stalwart woman member of the Labour Club started out innocently at a club social. Later we joined forces in a sport usually played indoors in the British climate. Choosing a park by the Cam, our enthusiasm outstripped even this harsh environment and I threw my clothes away so wildly that I never did find my socks.

The social evenings of the Canada Club were active but not as lusty. The one woman member was excluded as being too shockable. One meeting ended in my rooms with the smaller items of furniture, including potties, lying among the resentful ducks in the Cam below my window. When I swore to the Lady Superintendent of the college that this would never happen again, she only lisped sceptically, "I wonder, Mr. Reece ... I wonder ... ."

A more genteel social setting opened to me in my last term or two when I became *persona grata* to a group of Newnham College girls who invited suitable males to tea. Newnham girls were more silk and less blue stocking than members of the only other female college at that time — Girton — where a red-handed chemist had been my chum. My pleasure at the Newnham invitations was spoiled finally by the greater attention they lavished on another Canadian who had just arrived at Cambridge. He was loud, uncouth, and uninhibited. At tea he sat on the floor clutching his knees, rocking back and forth and even crying out McGill college yells. I felt better when I realized that his popularity was entirely due to his fulfillment of the English upper-class misconception of the Canadian yuck. Three years of acclimatization to British ways had denied me first prize at Newnham.

The apex of social life at Cambridge was a series of college dances called the May Balls although all were in June after the exams. These affairs were in delightful contrast to the austere times. At one of them, with a young Canadian visitor aboard, I steered a punt quietly down the Cam to cool off after the dance floor. Suddenly, as we paused in a sliver of moonlight, a strong rhythmic vibration began against our prow from another punt bumping into us. The two inmates had short silver hair but whether they were man and woman, two men or two women, was not clear. Perhaps they were professors at play. I did not wish to know, particularly with a sweet innocent at my side. Shielding her from this rather grotesque spectacle, I punted swiftly downstream.

At my only other May Ball, I accompanied some American friends and visitors. After we had dined together we went on to the Ball. At the dinner I had been attracted by one of the young visitors. On our arrival at the Ball she shyly presented me with her dance program and carte blanche to book her for various dances. I crassly waved the program aside as irrelevant to my intended monopoly. But she quietly disappeared and filled up her program minus Reece with someone I angrily called a "gummy-eyed" Englishman. I found solace in teaching two other American student visitors the "Palais Glide," a fashionable dance of the time. I did so on the Trinity College footbridge, an ancient curving stonework. Never was dancing so badly taught in such a delightful ballroom! One of my partners on this unique and lovely dance floor became a successful author and social secretary in the White House. I doubt, however, that the "Palais Glide" was featured there.

My farewell social fling in Cambridge outweighed my total meagre hospitality of the previous three years. I shared a cocktail party with Cradock who was running for Union President while I was "going down" ... leaving. A jolly party but we ran out of gin and finished off with sherry, a gut-stirring mix. A gay little dinner party I hosted afterwards in a fancy restaurant I could not afford almost ended in disgrace as the mixed drinks rose swiftly through my internal plumbing. Sickness was imminent. How was I to escape gracefully from my guests? Divine intervention. A waiter appeared asking "Which of you young gentleman's gown is on fire?" "Mine, mine," I cried and plunged askew down the stairs to the coat rack. By god, it was too, with a cigarette in the lining. Throwing five pound notes at the providential waiter, I leapt into a cab and got back to my lodgings, by then on Saxon Street, just in time to rush through the front hall to the outhouse toilet in the back garden. Since I did not have the face to seek change afterwards from the elegant restaurant, it was not surprising that I had to sell my typewriter to pay my debts before leaving town.

CHAPTER FIVE

Odd Jobs and Hot Nights
(1949-52)

THE NEXT YEAR was grubby. A tedious job with a publishing firm in London founded by friends but confined by lack of capital to a narrow range of books sponsored by commercial companies. I was no good at either selling our services or laying out designs. My father had some quid in the firm, but I eventually got them back. It was a lesson once more in a no-no métier for me.

After a compressed trudge through the Bar exams using a friend's notes from a crammer's course which I could not myself afford, I found a delightful job with the English Speaking Union. My duties included organizing large meetings for our membership. Two Canadian friends who were freelance journalists in London were worthy and well-paid contributors to the ESU house organ which aspired, successfully, to be a magazine of general topical interest. (I was its assistant editor.) But when the same friend produced for one issue an article and drawings to illustrate someone else's piece, I decided a pseudonym would be desirable. My friends also picked up the odd free meal since I was allowed to include outside guests when I dined the speakers after a small weekly meeting which I convened and chaired. I thus felt benevolent if not affluent. My pay was five hundred pounds a year, then about fifteen hundred Canadian dollars. With some regret I had passed up three hundred pounds a year to teach at a grammar school in South Ealing. Young Mr. Chips might have been fun for a year, teaching almost everything except science.

In the summer of '47 Loch Lomond was the delightful, even sunny, back-drop to a UN student seminar I attended. Alas for these bucolic delights and a buxom delegate from Birmingham: the far Left sought to dominate the seminar and win support for pro-Soviet postures. I reluctantly absent-ed myself from the lakeside to combat their knavish tricks, since no one else seemed to care much that twisted sentiments from our seminar could be blazoned abroad as U.K. student opinion. I was fairly successful even-tually in obtaining balanced resolutions despite able opposition.

Since my Department of Veterans' Affairs grant did not nearly cover Cambridge costs and my father's pocket was not deep, I did a span of hol-iday jobs, including the graveyard shift at Waterloo Station heaving mail sacks. My companions were a fascist dental student and a Trotskyite archi-tecture undergraduate. With a little amiable bickering between the oppo-site poles, they were genial companions of the night.

But my most lucrative and entertaining short labour stints were in the Kent hop fields along with two dozen other Oxbridge graduates hand-picked by a brewing company personnel officer. He was a very pukka retired major. Perhaps because I had listed "walking" as a hobby, an un-American sport in those days, he made me one of two camp foremen. This duty was not of crushing weight because the work required of this effete band of students was spasmodic and pleasant. Morale and discipline were not problems. We did not pick hops by hand, nothing so low. Legions of East-Enders were camped around the brewers' hop farms to do that. We undergraduates pulled down the hop bines (vines) and dumped them onto handcarts which conveyed them to the hop-picking machines. We then fed them into these rather bizarre apparati. There were two kinds, both imper-fect. One used steel combs pulled on a moving belt, but half of the acorn-shaped sticky hops stuck on the combs. The other machine used steel fin-gers which failed to tickle off about 40 percent of the hops. Both broke down frequently. When they did not work, we did not. It was a lazy sum-mer. I read a lot of Virginia Woolf.

But the company persisted. They hired more of us the next year. Some were from London University. At first the pattern was unchanged: same breakdowns, same golden summer, same paid leisure. A departing Polish refugee student hailed me as a "born leader," a heartwarming cliché. Since he was wearing jackboots at the time, I was impressed. But chaos set in this time. The London students pulled up flower pots in the hostel grounds and hurled them at one another. My disciplinary powers waned. The next year the hop farm manager never even acknowledged two letters from me seeking a third summer job. And I really needed the money.

The ripest summer was 1949. My hop feeding stint that year was after a month in Europe. My six-year stretch in England was not rich in foreign travel — lack of finance. But this trip was the exception. With two comrades I plunged like an uncorked zephyr into a mini-Grand Tour — Paris, Rome, and Florence. One friend was a Canadian from Ravenscourt days, Rowland Williams, and the other my colleague and union friend, Percy Cradock. His erudition equalled his formidable grey matter. He had even read Ruskin on Florence. We stopped first to sup the delights of Paris. These were concentrated for me in a Canadian girl who was staying with family friends. They were wine producers of venerable vintage and a household name. I was invited to dine in their enormous apartment which overwhelmed the modest student with its sweeping inner staircase down which the hostess swept, and with its butler and the infinite disdain with which he accepted my tawdry raincoat. The family meal was a shade stiff but warmed a little by generous draughts of a non-vintage wine from the family vineyards served before, after, and during the dinner. The next day I called on my friend of the heart only to find that all were at the Longchamps race meet. I did not follow them. My raincoat was decidedly not Longchamps.

Shaking off these glimpses of haut-bourgeois life we three took the train to Rome. Unfortunately we took the wrong train. It took us through Switzerland, not the Riviera, to Italy. Swiss ticket punchers were alive to this. Since none of our ticket price went to the Swiss railways and here we were chuffing through their country, they popped in on us at every stop seeking their share and in Swiss francs too. They never got it. We sang the same refrain each time. We were poor students and it was not our fault we were put on the wrong train in Paris. The latter assertion was shakier than the former. At the first stop in Italy a full-blooded attempt was made on our purse in lire. We were hauled off the train. A tousled station master appeared. We speculated romantically that he had just been hauled out of his mistress's bed. He heard our song with cynical weariness and then let us get back on the train. Presumably he wanted to go back to her bed.

Thus we arrived in Rome in cheerful triumph. Our hotel, the Albergo Rex, was not in fact fit for royalty nor a king among hotels, but it did have a close-up view of a seething market. We threw money to the Roman breeze on our last night, after a spartan three days, and dined at Ulpia's, a magnificent restaurant I have never afforded since. Then off to the open air opera in the ancient Roman baths amidst cries of "multo tardo." It was good to swagger in on a scene thundering with mezzo sopranos and live elephants in *La Forza del Destino*.

And so to Florence. A slower pace but louder, car whines overridden by the first generation of motor scooters belching racket and fume. Ignoring this aberration, we did our pleasant duty in galleries, museums, and churches in the morning, drank hoggishly of rotgut wine at lunch, deeply observed the siesta, then did a bit more culture in the cooled off period. At night more wine. In general we spent more money on liquids than solids, although I learned to eat spaghetti with fork-twirling nonchalance.

Just when our money was touching bottom, another former Cambridge friend appeared, John Noonan, an American who became a legal scholar and a senior U.S. judge. He watered our financial drought by buying our copy of a standard history of the Medici, a thick work worth three days at a villa in Fiesole. (Noonan, my wife and I visited this cool and lovely spot thirty-six years later.)

Holidays on the Continent were then still reached mainly by channel ferries, especially if you were young and straitened. Having been deeply seasick in the Navy, I was radiant to graduate finally from that cursed class one stormy summer day in 1952. I had dosed myself with two seasick pills followed by two large whiskies in the main lounge of a corkscrewing channel boat. Far from being laid low by this stiff mixture and the cocktail shaker rhythm of the boat, I felt very chipper. The more so because many of my fellow loungers were sick — to the extent that the bathrooms were full up and the later victims reduced to paper bags *in situ*. My sadistic glow grew at the sight of a burly Olympic team throwing up in all directions. They had won a gold medal. No medal now.

I left the sordid crowd below in the main lounge and moved up to the bar where I joined a crass English commercial traveller who was enjoying the suffering of others as much as I. The ship's captain joined us and remarked that there was a "bit of a blow" that day as we savoured our drinks in the deserted bar. Graduation indeed.

One high point of my London social life in 1951 was what became famous in a very small circle as "Jimmy's Wet Nurse Party." The host had spent a congenial convalescence in a London nursing home and wished to repay kindness. He also wanted to have a lively party. He shared a house of square ample cut with two other bachelors. He included in his guest list every would-be swinging bachelor he knew. I was one. The three-storey house was divided into an inoculation room on the ground floor, a pre-op room on the second floor, and an operating theatre on the top floor. The female guests were nurses in their twenties and a few like-minded friends. Masked and gowned figures led by a lean Oxford don inoculated them with strong dry martinis at the front door. The second floor was for dancing and the third for, well, operations. Deep couches were in attendance.

The hinge of the year '51-'52 was comic and slightly violent. I had been invited to a New Year's Eve party by a whimsical and talented freelance journalist friend from Canada, Ken Black, who had passed his happiest summer driving a team of husky dogs in the Festival of Britain in 1951. He had arranged to have the party in someone else's premises, a studio belonging to a pair of Marxist artists called Bones and Jones. Thither I invited a young Canadian actress, Frances Hyland, who was playing with skill and bite a juvenile lead in a West End play. Chagrin at the stage door. The doorman told me she had left after the play with no message for me. Mixed signals. In fact, she was still in the theatre having a drink in the leading lady's dressing room. As midnight approached at the party I made a last shot phone call to her lodgings and found her there, equally cross with me. After urging her to take a taxi, I then decided, after hanging up, that this was very unlikely to be feasible. A cool solicitor at the party offered to drive me. When we reached her house the bird had flown to Bones and Jones in a taxi.

On the way back there we were stopped by a joyous crowd who had spilled out of a pub in lower Hammersmith. After they had sung "Auld

Lang Syne" and had started to recede from the crossroads, I urged the driver to move on. Visions of charming Frances tumbled in my head like sugar plums. As soon as we started forward the crowd surged back. We knocked down, rather gently, an old man and a fish-wife type. The old man rose slowly, but the woman began screaming bloody murder! Instantly the crowd's mood leapt from drunken amiable to drunken angry. A beefy fist came through my open car window knocking out a tooth and blackening my eye. I remonstrated and pleaded. This uncorked a roar of "They're Americans — get 'em!" Unhappily I was still clutching an empty glass in my hand: "They're drunk, the bastards, get 'em!" After an age and some car rocking a lone constable arrived. He wisely moved us some distance from the turbulence. The driver fortunately remained cool and sober. Having locked his door and closed his window, he had not received any corporal punishment. An angry crowd followed us. One truculent citizen demanded our arrest and punishment. The cop invited him to come to the police station and lay a charge. "Argh, I don't go for police stations," he said as he faded into the night.

Our arrival at the party was seasoned with relief and a small dash of wounded heroship. But our tale of adventure was twisted in the years to come by our host's jesting apocryphal version as follows. As a former executive of the Cambridge Labour Club, I had assured my solicitor friend, "I can handle this — with my experience I can manage these people — I know their psychology." At that moment the fist sailed through the window!

Another New Year's Eve a few young Canadians and I gate-crashed the Chelsea Arts Ball. Accompanied by decorous young English girls and after a decorous dance elsewhere we surged into the Albert Hall at 2:00 A.M. Resistance was not encountered. Everyone seemed nine sheets to the wind. It is the only occasion I have seen where couples fell over on the dance floor and did not get up again. Figures dressed in Tudor costume sat in boxes and threw gnawed chicken bones to the throbbing crowd below. Henry VIII could have done no better. Tiring eventually of this brightly-robed bacchanalia, we dropped off our proper young ladies and retreated to our seamy hotel. But even here we caroused so noisily that we were chucked out. Happily one of us, David McQueen, later an eminent economic functionary and scholar but then a scruffy student at the London

School of Economics, had nearby rooms where we sheltered until the turkish baths opened. It seems our behaviour lacked polish once again because McQueen's landlady noted to him next day, "You 'ad Mr. Hitler in there last night. I 'eard you!"

A more worthy activity of our group of temporary Canadian ex-pats in London that winter was literary criticism. Six or seven of us met every month to hear a paper from one of us on some contemporary novelist. Symptomatically no Canadian writer was tackled. Not all the learning was solemn. One presentation included a faked interview on tape with Graham Greene. Never did he sound so creative. My own paper on "The Novels of F. Scott Fitzgerald" was trenchantly criticized by two English friends I had invited to join us. Stung but unscathed I sent a revised version to a British journal of letters and political studies. They published it and overwhelmed me with a payment of three guineas plus twelve free copies. However, such was my erudition, authority and vast knowledge of the subject that I had mislettered Fitzgerald's name with a big G instead of a small one. The journal caught this just in time to print the name correctly on the cover of their monthly issue but not in the text of the article. They did not take back my fee but I decided against being a professional critic. I gave away all my copies.

The only other time I have written and published in the realm of literature was a brief book revue for the *Surge*, the "Magazine of Youth," in New Delhi in 1955. Needless to say we humorous youth called it *Urge* to the fury of its serious-minded editor, a comely Indian maiden. I received no fee this time.

CHAPTER SIX

External Affairs, Ottawa, and India
(1952-57)

IN ENGLAND, after a scholarly vocation evaporated and the law and politics stultified, I turned my thoughts to the foreign service with hope and a touch of desperation. This was a period when Canadian foreign policy under Lester Pearson was on the move. Canada's work on the foundations and early structure of the United Nations and NATO was substantial and acknowledged. Our small élite of diplomats needed helpers in a growing task. External seemed glamorous but solid.

Annual competitions for entry were held in major foreign capitals as well as across Canada. Few were picked from the many. NATO and Pearson unwittingly helped me to make it. NATO's initial headquarters were in London where I had a friend in the Secretariat. The library door was open to me and there I found, by chance, an article on Canadian foreign policy by Pearson in the learned U.S. publication *Foreign Affairs*. The three-hour essay paper, which was part of the exam for External in 1951, listed Canadian foreign policy as one of the optional topics. I chose it and drew neatly but not completely on the Pearson text. Making use of the maestro ....

Luck also played a favourable hand in the second stage of the competition, the interview. This took place at Canada House with three interlocutors who seemed to have had a stimulating lunch. I struck some rapport with one, a seasoned diplomat who was attuned to the British political and literary scene. Drawing on the *New Statesman and Nation* and the beefier Sunday papers, I made bright answers. (I had made a point of describing in my application form my very active student political involvement in the left-wing British Labour Party. If this was to make any difference in those harsh cold war days, I would rather stay out. It did not.)

The third and last hoop was a discussion group. We were divided into sets of four with a chairman from the Civil Service Commission. We discussed the acute and insoluble problems not of the UN or NATO but of a fictitious Arctic community. The interviewers sat within earshot. One candidate in my group came over as brash and egregious; the rest of us must have glittered a little by comparison. The final result was twenty-four new foreign service officers, three of them women, recruited that year. The order of placement was leaked to some of us from the personnel division. I had placed ninth. I may have crept a little higher by the end of my career.

When I joined up in September, 1952, the Department of External Affairs, the Prime Minister's Office, and the Privy Council Office were all housed in the stately and gothicized East Block on Parliament Hill in Ottawa. The so-called "University of the East Block," provided some briefing sessions, but our training consisted mainly of exposure to work in some of the various divisions. Mine began in the Americas Division (now grown to several), which was interesting, and in the Legal Division where I caused displeasure by making plain my dislike of legal work.

Having narrowly survived my probationary period, I then hit it lucky as Executive Assistant to the Under-Secretary of State for External Affairs (USSEA), the civil service head of the department — equivalent to deputy minister. There are now, of course, more people in that office. They are doubtless busy as moles, but in my day there was little to do beyond sieving the paper aimed at the boss. This gave me a bird's-eye view of the service, valuable to a neophyte, but I found it hard to answer the sardonic query of one senior officer as to what the bird actually thought of what he did see. The scene was enlivened by officials bursting in with hot telegrams and memos demanding immediate attention by the All High. Many of these dealt with the Korean War where Canada and our Minister, Lester B. Pearson, were playing a valuable role in the long agony of peacemaking.

One high advantage of this job was its daily contact with the USSEA. For a short period of my time there, Dana Wilgress was in office, a wise, balanced, and practical man. Then it was Charles Ritchie, as Acting USSEA, who was a delightful taskmaster with an acute intelligence self-concealed by sallies and laughter. My next stint was in the United Nations Division where I sent long, turgid, but worthy telegrams to our UN delegation in New York about the plight of left-wing American citizens whose jobs in the UN Secretariat were being threatened by McCarthyite pressure from within and outside the U.S. administration. My home life, so to speak, in this period was based in the house of Mrs. Katy McLaine, a widow who provided rooms for three fortunate young men along with bumper breakfasts and the sauce of her kindly wit.

My first posting abroad literally was an accident. I was sent to New Delhi to replace an officer who had to be shipped back to Canada because of injuries suffered in a car crash. I felt at home in Asia from the first pungent smell at Istanbul airport. India in 1954 was a fierce but enchanting place.

In spite of the cooking climate eight months of the year, Delhi was a gold mine of experience for any young diplomat who could stand driving at over 100 degrees inside his car. No car air conditioners then. The central machine in the office often broke down for sweaty stretches at a time. Electric fans blew the papers all over the room. Civil servants like to shuffle papers but not at electric whim. A shrewd and humorous colleague often worked sitting under his desk. It was not just a joke. The papers stayed still while the refracted air from the ceiling fan provided some cool. Otherwise the sweat ran down your arms onto your pen and paper. A damp dispatch.

It was tough, challenging, and enormously compelling to be in post-independence India, Nehru's India. The hope level was rising. The Green Revolution was still ten years ahead and the British Raj's red tape bureaucratic style was still strangulating but there was energy radiating from the top. Nehru was viceroy now but Harrow and Cambridge had not stifled the Indian. He was a princely democrat. A figure of mercurial charm. But too dominant. Decisions were concentrated on his desk to a stagnating degree.

I saw a comic example of this domination combined with a magnificent *faux pas* at a dinner party given by the High Commissioner. The dinner marked the signing of a Canada-India aid agreement to build a research reactor, the one said later to have supplied the plutonium for India's

atomic bomb — or peaceful explosion if you prefer — in 1974. As the
junior organizer for the event, I was placed at the remote outer edge of the
huge table. When the women withdrew for coffee — a British custom still
unquestioned — Nehru and the High Commissioner conducted a one-
sided dialogue for the edification of the other guests; Indian cabinet ministers, senior civil servants, scientists, and Canadian officials. My boss' task
was to ask a few questions. Finally Nehru said, "Well, you know, they keep
coming to me for all sorts of decisions, big and small. The other day the
government of Punjab came to me about its new capital city which is being
designed by Le Corbusier. He wants to create a symbolic monument to
stand on the hillside above the new city. It is to be a giant hand. How —
they even ask me this — how should the hand go — upraised, facing left,
facing right?" Forgetting, we assume, that the dinner was celebrating an
important aid agreement with Canada, one of our officers leaned across the
table, extended his own hand forward, palm up like a beggar and suggested, "The hand should certainly not be like this!" This supremely tactless
gambit may have resulted from the frustration of being ignored throughout the meal while sitting next to Krishna Menon. Menon, the sardonic
confidant of Nehru whom some thought an evil influence, had also eaten
almost nothing, perhaps to torture the hostess who had provided his
favourite dishes. Whatever caused the gaffe, Nehru kept talking unper-
turbed while Reece, sitting well below the salt, almost burst with sup-
pressed mirth.

When Nehru left after dinner, the embargo on alcohol was lifted. Trays
of drink swooped in. Cabinet ministers chuckled about mice playing
minus the cat. In general the social ambiance of Delhi was still tinged with
Raj rather than Gandhi. We even wore dinner jackets to the umpteen cocktail parties. The stately Gymkhana Club had every hallmark of the former
rulers. Except that foreigners had to wait a long time to become members.

Escott Reid, the High Commissioner, had retained his cool during the
dinner party hand misfeasance and his undoubted horror may have been
watered with secret chuckles. He was — and is — a witty man. I was very
lucky to have had him as my first "guru" and wrote him so when he was
made a Companion of the Order of Canada in 1971. He was intense, indus-
trious, exigent, and sometimes unreasonable, but, if he liked your flavour,

you were given much rope and long rein. He taught me how to write political and economic reports. He cut my long wind and long sentences. He encouraged enthusiasm. He improved my social graces. As a convenient bachelor, I was chucked into official dinners as filler for the table plans I myself had to concoct. The mathematical almost metaphysical art of drawing up a table plan conforming to the rules of precedence while putting interesting people usefully beside each other was an enduring skill of protocol acquired on my first posting and used to the very last dinner of my career. Too many times I suffered the ham-fisted lack of such a skill at other diplomats' tables.

More substantially, Escott, as I did not call him then, saw to it that I had every variety of solid and intriguing chore in the office, starting with administrative and consular duties and graduating to political and economic reporting and public affairs. He sent me travelling around India to learn India. As much as possible in a diplomatic setting, a rapport grew between us, I believe, fed by our shared Oxbridge experiences and our left-liberal perspectives.

Reid's liberalism and deep concern about conditions in India, his swift, sometimes blazing intelligence, put him ahead, sometimes harmfully ahead, of more plebeian minds in Ottawa. For example, he pressed for the idea of tied lines of credit, new flexible loans and commodity grants from the Canadian government which, determined by the recipient government, would produce the most effect where most needed while encouraging Canadian exports. This was too much for Ottawa's aid/economic community to swallow. Their thinking then seemed fixed on conventional projects and technical assistance. They have since become more flexible.

Escott also outpaced Ottawa on the overlapping Suez and Hungary crises. He thought Canada's role crucial in sustaining important western links with India and influencing them on Hungary despite Suez. The U.K. had, for the moment, lost its standing with India which was outraged by the Suez adventure. (In November, 1956, despite a U.N. resolution for a cessation of hostilities, Britain and France followed up a prior bombing raid by sending troops into the Suez Canal area. This was done in reaction to Egyptian President Nasser's earlier takeover of the predominantly Anglo-French Suez Canal Company, which had operated the Canal since

1869.) The effect of the more congenial U.S. attitude on Suez was much diminished by long-standing strains over U.S. friendship with Pakistan and India's with the Soviet Union. Since the two major Western powers were largely without influence over India at that point, Canada had a much increased responsibility. And India was of vital weight in the balance of non-aligned and world reaction to Soviet brutality in Hungary. So argued Escott in telegrams too hot and many for Ottawa, and in *démarches* skilled and sustained with Indian policy makers. He was eventually told bluntly to lay off. But not before he had used his contacts and standing to notable effect on the Indian position on Hungary.

Ottawa's role was usually more helpful. Escott's ability and brilliant work for Canada-India cooperation were fully recognized. Although Canada was far away and had a relatively small aid program, we were forging bilateral and Commonwealth ties of increasing strength. Reid's relations with Indian ministers and senior officials were a model of diplomatic skill and congeniality. This was crystallized in his friendship with the charming and subtle top official in the foreign ministry, Raghavan Pillai. In the Suez-Hungary affair this link of mutual appreciation and admiration was a key element in Canadian influence and was a continuing factor of value in the work of the High Commission.

Although he had to comply with Ottawa's wishes when it came to a crunch, Escott rarely accepted total defeat. This was illustrated in a case I knew well, a raid on his staff. In 1954 my widowed mother had rented her flat in England for three months to stay with me in Delhi. She had just arrived when a telegram came from Ottawa posting me to Laos for two months *sans délai* to fill a gap in our delegation to the international commission there. Escott replied that this would be unfair in the circumstances and was told to send another officer in my place immediately. Since the only two other officers then in Delhi had family responsibilities, albeit of less short-term nature than mine, Escott sent them one after the other for one month.

Escott should have become our man in London and Washington and the Under-Secretary in Ottawa. These were his legitimate ambitions. But distrust of zeal outweighed admiration. His career continued, however, with distinction and variety, as Ambassador in Bonn, senior official with the

External Affairs Minister L.B. Pearson and High Commissioner Reid laying wreaths in New Delhi, 1955. David in the back row.

World Bank, the first Principal of Glendon College at York University, and as author of seven books.

Ruth Reid matched her husband's good looks, charm, and humour. She told a story on herself about my blunt and candid predecessor on Escott's staff whom Ruth herself nursed day and night in the Residence after the car accident. Finally the patient began to show improvement and some interest in life. To encourage this, Ruth ran down the plans and guest list for a dinner chez Reid that evening. "Humph," was the response — "it sounds just as boring as all your dinner parties!"

A men's lunch for visiting Canadians I attended at the Residence was not at all boring. (A Residence is the official home, owned by the Canadian government, of the head of mission — Ambassador, High Commissioner, or Consul General). The guests were three leaders of missionary organisations and an engineer who had been providing technical assistance in Indonesia and Bengal. The missionaries had just been in West Africa and with horror and relish told stories of superstitious rites seen there. "Well," said the engineer, "I was reared in a Mohawk long house myself and I've seen some very superstitious rites in Christian churches, like sprinkling holy water with mumbo jumbo on new bridges in Quebec."

Canada's relations with the new India were stimulated during my posting by visits from External Affairs Minister Pearson in 1955 and Health and Welfare Minister Paul Martin in 1956. Since the Pearson visit was my first of any importance, I prepared mounds of paper for it, programs in three dimensions, and a wealth of background briefing. I then received a sharp lesson in priorities from Mrs. Pearson. She brushed aside all this tedious bumph and demanded the whereabouts of her personal mail. So I scaled down the paper for the Martin visit. He was so entranced by the hefty size and attentiveness of the village audiences which he addressed through interpreters in the area around Delhi that he returned to us in a state of dazed delight and political euphoria. The Indians knew how to please visitors.

My own first visit outside New Delhi included a week in a village house, sleeping with a dozen others on string beds as the guest of a Canadian research student probing the obstacles to increasing agricultural output in India. The nub seemed to be too much cheap labour from the untouchables and too much idleness from their employers, caste Hindus.

The tropical green and sweaty humidity of South India were always a change from Delhi, whether in its summer furnace phase or its crisp and sparkling winter. My first trip south was by air-conditioned train. (Escott had heard lurid stories, no doubt over-coloured, of the maintenance practices on Indian planes.) The train compartments, which were steel cold, had two bunks. The railway authorities allotted them with sexual indiscrimination. The Canadian government therefore bought both bunks to protect staff travelling alone. Perhaps this caution was the result of an episode some years earlier when one of our officers unwittingly booked his wife into a four-bunk compartment. He is said to have made a scene flapping down the station platform with alarm as the train pulled out, his wife and her three mates, large and smiling Indian males, enjoying his noisy indignation. My own journey was a chilly bore. At every stop as we rocked down the centre of India, I jumped onto the platform and into surging crowds searching for humanity and warmth. Then back into my solo icebox where I munched chicken from my cook's hamper. At least the scenery was vivid and often beautiful during a long two days.

During this southern journey I made a side trip to see a Christian hospital where there were some Canadian staff. A Canadian resident in Madras came with me, an elegant blonde. Her British husband insisted we travel in one of his company cars rather than use a local taxi of unknown stripe. In the event our safety was not assured. On a stretch of rain wet road, our driver went too fast and neatly turned us on our side after a circular skid. We were not hurt but my companion was a bit shaken. She went down the road to relieve stress and bladder in some wayside bushes. A bus appeared from the other direction. The driver and passengers craned to look at the blonde. This lapse of attention resulted in a similar skid and the bus turned onto its side. Again no injuries but ironic laughter from us. We eventually resumed our trip in another company car with a more prudent driver.

At the hospital we were shocked by the task of a young Canadian psychiatrist. She was trying to combat and cure serious mental illness on an out-patient basis. There was no room in the hospital for a ward for her patients. They stayed with relatives in small nearby hotels, violent cases chained to the bed. The young doctor was almost in despair.

More cheerful was the lepers' ward. They were now curable or at least arrestable with new drugs. They were in any case said to be more cheerful by disposition as an ironic side-effect of their affliction. Later on that trip, at a river crossing in Kerala, I saw a sight more grisly than any in the leper ward. On a hand cart a horrible victim of God knows what diseases lay with tangled limbs, triangular head, and distorted features. He was being exploited by his handlers to beg money from the rotating captive audience who had to wait for the ferry. Yes, I gave him something.

Another selfless Canadian I met on the trip was a man on the upper slopes of middle age, Wallace Forgie. He lived in spartan conditions as the organizer and director of a boys' camp outside Madras. He had been there for some years and had no intention of giving up a role of difficulty and limited scope but of direct human value.

On another trip I lunched with a pleasant British couple who ran an estate near a town south of Madras. They were among the few such British survivors in that area. The wife mentioned at lunch, with a silvery laugh, that they had been warned against having a garden (flowers and shrubs) because it was a magnet and shelter for snakes. As I could see through the abundant windows of the bungalow, the advice had been lavishly ignored. My hosts loved gardens. After lunch as I stepped out the door I met the hostess who looked as if she had been practising chip shots with a number nine iron. Then I looked at her feet. They were in the process of kicking away a snake which had just died from the golf club. It was a highly poisonous Russell's viper. I was glad I had not accepted her invitation to stay the night.

During a later stay in Madras City I was reminded of a feature which I had ignored before. Madras was "dry ... very dry." Foreigners were allowed to get permits from the police as "addicts." Since my highly respectable mother was with me, I decided we should obey the law. Accompanied by this dignified, and rather amused, mother figure, I went down to the police station only to find the permit section closed. So we went back to the hotel and continued to drink from our mobile supply. Bombay was almost as dry. After a lavish lunch festooned with wine I was taken to the liquor permit office by our resident trade commissioner. I held my breath.

Indian girls were a problem for foreign bachelor diplomats. The educated and interesting ones were the daughters of senior officials whom it was our duty to please. A sure way to displease them was to pursue their daughters. In the '50s such parents did not like foreigners messing around with their well-bred flowers who were supposed to make an appropriate marriage with the son of some other senior official. The girls had all been at Miranda House of Delhi University and the acceptable boys to the Doon School modelled predictably on British public schools. So what to do? Happily I struck up a pleasant friendship with a young Indian couple used to foreigners. The wife, an artist and classical singer of eventual distinction, had the *sine qua non* key. She had been to Miranda House. The couple's modern outlook and tolerance was partly based on their mixed marriage. She was a caste Hindu and he a Christian. More importantly, his family were Muslim one step back. This couple kindly made up a foursome for a few agreeable outings with one or other of two Miranda House graduates I favoured. Nothing serious ever seemed imminent although my married Indian friend was sufficiently concerned at one stage to note to me the problems involved in inter-communal marriages. The hint was unnecessary.

I may, however, have missed a maternal hint. At a farewell party for me given by the more reserved of the two Miranda House girls her mother tut-tutted that "Poor Sushila — my mother was married when she was nine and I at sixteen and Sushila is unwed at twenty-three." I mentally noted that the girl would have married long since if her parents had not insisted that any husband be of the same sub-caste of Brahmins. It was months later when a possible penny dropped in my innocent mind. Maybe mamma was desperate enough to have been waiving all caste and colour bars that night, if indeed Sushila (not her name) would have put up with me. She married quite soon afterwards an Indian not of her caste or geographic community.

The more ebullient Miranda House girl actually permitted me to embrace her once lightly in the lane behind her house. She instantly declared that this was a trivial Western custom equivalent to eating ice cream. Not very complimentary. A shy young Indian woman alarmed me in Kashmir. She rubbed my feet gently after dinner. Then I remembered that this was an ancient Indian custom. I relaxed and fell innocently asleep.

There were, of course, many foreign women in India. One from the West German Embassy allowed me to take her out in return for listening to bitter and justified complaints about the merciless and pointless bombing of her birthplace, Dresden, in 1945. I discovered I was a mere stop-gap when her steady boyfriend returned from leave in Europe. Then an exotic Ceylonese girl preferred a White Russian fur merchant and an American anthropologist asked to meet the mother, then visiting me, who had bred this curious Canadian. A lively American secretary opted for a Marine officer. Happily there were two or three English girls who provided tea and sympathy. Among the remaining ex-pats in Delhi, bankers, insurance executives, merchants, and even dentists, charming daughters could be found. (I had my rocky fangs maintained, however, by an Indian dentist trained at McGill.) Apart from the local maidens, Indians in general were quite easy to befriend. Language was no hindrance. In fact, accents of different twang in English were an attraction.

I was too junior to be used for solo discussions in the foreign ministry at the level of influence but I did accompany more senior Canadian officers on occasion. I did meet socially some young officials of interest and charm.

And one of my few solo calls on the ministry was to seek background information on the new Indian system of decorations for worthy citizens. Thus I had an early hand in the shaping of our own honours system.

My duties as information and press officer as well as my reporting chores made media men and women obvious prey for cultivation. In the absence of any resident Canadian correspondents I made do nicely with a cluster of British and American journalists. They included Louis Heren of the *Times* and Abe Rosenthal of the other *Times* in New York. Both later rose to the top of their newspaper hierarchies. Both were sprightly characters. Congenial Indian newsmen included the perky G.K. Reddy of the *Times of India*, and the intellectually dapper but very serious George Verghese, an Oxbridge Anglican from Punjab, who served for a time as Prime Minister Indira Gandhi's press secretary. K. Rangaswami and D.R. Mankekar were two kindly senior journalists who helped to enlighten a junior Canadian. A sage from an older generation was Sri Krishna, an economic journalist. He was prepared to lay bare for me the base motives and inwardness of any situation, political, economic, or scandalous. A delightful old man who seemed to me a well of all Indian wisdom, deeply mellow if flavoured with caustic scepticism. I once spent a rugged evening with the senior editor and well-known author, Frank Moraes, who was a heavyweight in every sense. He was in a mood of vinous venom against the West and its knavish tricks. I had to contest his more extreme barbs but it was prickly work.

These contacts with the press enabled both sides to share views, titbits, and insights. The journalists had stories unfit to print and I could occasionally provide a discreet slant. It was good early training in the diplomat's tightrope of relations with the press. But once I fell off and mislaid all discretion over a cool scotch in a hot garden. Too late I found myself relaying to the editor of a national economic weekly the gist of recommendations given to Escott Reid and myself that day by an international economist of towering reputation. He had been employed by the Indian government to make suggestions to them about planning and development. He underlined to us that his views were for our ears (and Ottawa's) only. And here I had blabbed them to the Indian press! The next morning I stewed over my ridiculous but grave indiscretion. Then I recalled with pure panic that I had arranged a lunch for Escott which included the economist, the editor, and myself. This would surely stimulate my unmasking as a master leaker before my thunderstruck boss. In any case the revelations to be expected in the weekly would be easily traceable to me. I desperately grasped the nettle. I phoned the editor and explained that I had inadvertently breached a confidence. I would be most grateful if he could treat whatever he heard from me as deep background at most. I mentioned the lunch hoping this might be an inducement (i.e., he would be able to do his own digging). The editor sounded rather stunned and made vague noises only. But not a word appeared on the subject. Either he took pity on me or did not think the stuff was worth mentioning in his journal. Then I phoned Escott and begged off the lunch on the grounds of volatile dysentery. Thus a true leak ended in a false dysentery.

My best friends in India were a Canadian couple, Michael and Eva Brecher. Michael was on leave from teaching at McGill University. Eva, who was a Sabra, had been a member of the embryo Israeli army which fought in the 1948 war and then a diplomat in the new Israeli Embassy in Turkey. In Delhi she presided over two very small daughters and an apartment in Joe Fonseca's genial residential hotel next to the Canadian High Commission. Mike was doing research for a biography of Nehru. Although written in the mid-stream of Nehru's span of power, it remains the best study of this compelling leader.

The Brechers were warmly hospitable to a sometimes uncertain and frustrated bachelor. This even extended to letting me read Mike's letters from lively parts of India when he was touring with Nehru. Tasty morsels for my reports. Mike also showed me hot from the typewriter draft chapters on Nehru as they emerged. I made a few style and content suggestions. When the book was published Mike wanted a specific kind reference to my help in his acknowledgements page but the cruel czar of personnel in External Affairs refused on the grounds that the book might displease the Pakistan or Indian governments or both. Thus the kind reference is there but to "one who prefers to be anonymous." Like hell. I would have been proud to be named as lending a hand to a valuable book. The personnel chief pointed out to me, chuckling blackly, that the reference which did appear could apply to one or more other people! Bah.

Mike retained his connection with India for some years and produced other valuable works about India and its leaders followed by important books on the Middle East and world crises. He also invented and sparked into life the Indo-Canadian Shastri Institute for scholarly exchanges between the two countries. The Brechers are close friends still.

Three of my High Commission colleagues were helpful friends and superb diplomats. Along with Escott, they gave me a remarkably upmarket impression of calibre in Canadian posts — not confirmed 100 percent in all subsequent missions. The second-ranking official in a Canadian diplomatic post may have the designation of Minister, Minister Counsellor, Deputy High Commissioner, or Counsellor depending on the site of the post. Then follow the other officers in rank: First, Second, and Third Secretary. In New Delhi for my first year, the second official, the Counsellor, was Bruce Williams. He was shrewd, tough when necessary, but by preference, genial. A crisply effective manager, he had a gift for what is now called on officer rating forms "interpersonal relations." Patient with the apprentice Reece, he was a kind and sensitive son to his elderly mother who was in Delhi with him. Bruce had an acute ear and taste for gossip. Little of scandalous or political import escaped his antennae.

First Secretary McGaughey — "McGuff" — a humorist with a practical bent, was very much at home in a country and job of rich variety. His cheerful personality, at once subtle and hearty, was a boon to colleagues and Indian contacts. Escott valued his judgement. His charming wife Jessie, sympathetic regulator of two lively sons as well as her husband's expansiveness, ran a household which was always attractive and welcoming to a footloose bachelor. The McGuffs went on to a successful quadrilateral of posts as head of mission, making good use of their versatile skills. They retired a few years early because, as he put it, "the give and take of working for External Affairs were no longer agreeably in balance." The McGuffs swam into a fruitful new life including talented oil painting and witty correspondence.

Klaus Goldschlag, the Second Secretary, who covered the work now spread over large economic and aid sections, was an exceptional officer. He and his wife "Shan" were helpful to the green Third Secretary who was setting up house for the first time in a gritty little apartment. Klaus, quiet, neat, and intensely inquisitive, could and did run intellectual rings around us but never to our discomfort. To hear him and Bruce dissect a local political imbroglio and stitch it together with insight was good learning material. Never deeply malicious, Klaus's wit was sharp on target. He described with glee the papal nuncio at the Goldschlag's shipboard table who declared in harsh accents that their young daughter had "a will of iron ... it must be crushed!" Klaus's performance in Delhi in an overloaded job with an exigent boss was act one of a brilliant career at the top level of our service in Ottawa and at three ambassadorial posts. He was Deputy Under-Secretary of the department in the '70s.

No account of life at a diplomatic post would be worthwhile if it did not emphasize the importance of the work of the administrative or "support staff" who are either rotational Canadians — secretaries, communicators, and clerks with varying security clearances — or local nationals from consultants, translators, and receptionists to cooks and drivers. These latter are called "locally-engaged staff" a rather ambiguous term with a matrimonial tinge. In New Delhi, in fact, two Canadian women married to Indians worked in our office as local clerks. Marjorie Sen, wife of an Indian army officer, and Helen Singh, married to a professor of politics at the University of New Delhi, were towers of efficiency and sustained expertise. They kept me afloat with their help in my first year in Delhi when I had consular and administrative responsibilities.

CHAPTER SEVEN

Ottawa, Marriage, and Malaysia
(1956-59)

I WAS POSTED to Ottawa in the autumn of 1956 and served there until January 1958. This period included three months of temporary duty back in India to replace my replacement who had fallen sick with hepatitis. This was not surprising since he had arrived in India's baking heat straight from two rugged years of duty in Indo-China. My job in Ottawa before and after this busy but agreeable escape from the Canadian winter, from November to February, was to spread myself across the second floor of the East Block. I was executive assistant to both the Minister, Mr. Pearson, and to the Under-Secretary, Jules Léger, around the corner and down the hall. I did a mix of tasks for each but the majority for Léger, a thoughtful francophone who told me his excellent English was a constant cutting across the grain. Since my English was facile and fluent if not sculptural, he asked me one Friday afternoon to write a fireside chat for television to be given by the Prime Minister, Louis St. Laurent, on the Sunday night in this late autumn of 1956. The subject was the twin but separate crises of Suez and Hungary. Our department was then so small and simple that we did not have a separate division or unit dealing with the Middle East. I interpreted my orders to cover both flanks of conflict and churned out a fairly respectable draft by Saturday noon.

On the Sunday morning a furious visitor descended on me in the office. It was Bob Ford, the head of the European Division, who understandably accused me of poaching. I took shelter behind my own version of my instructions and peace was restored in Ottawa, although not in Budapest and Suez. I hope Ford was not too disappointed when the *Globe and Mail* described Mr. St. Laurent's television address as "dull." The *Globe* was doubtless referring to the Suez part of the speech because it opposed Canadian policy there. Ford went on with his remarkable career including four ambassadorial assignments ending with seventeen years in Moscow as the West's leading envoy.

As executive assistant in both offices, I attended policy meetings in order to run errands afterwards rather than contribute much wisdom. One of the more tense meetings was about the United Nations Emergency Force (UNEF), the newborn peacekeeping force for the Middle East in the wake of the Suez War. UNEF gave the United Nations a fertile and sustained addition to its duties. External Affairs Minister Pearson was the author of this important and creative initiative, along with John Holmes, a senior official. (Holmes left External a few years later but in fact widened his contribution to Canadian foreign policy through public affairs and academic life.) The purpose of our meeting on UNEF was to make recommendations to Pearson about the Canadian contribution. Egypt had refused to accept a Canadian contingent, the Queen's Own Rifles, because of the royal title! It was argued at our meeting that we should not participate at all in view of the Egyptian insult to the authors of UNEF, whose existence was key to a peace Nasser badly needed. The counter view pointed out the bitter irony of excluding ourselves from the peacekeeping force inspired by Canada to help solve a deep international crisis. In the end we swallowed the insult and contributed logistic troops. This valuable input was repeated in later United Nations actions. Nasser had done Canada and the United Nations a favour.

I accompanied Mr. Pearson to Bonn and London in the spring of 1957 for a NATO foreign ministers' meeting and then a conference of Canadian envoys posted in Europe. Both events were important in the light of the divisions still rankling in the wake of Suez. My role was largely bag-carrier and administrator. Not really my forte. I left both our passports behind in the safe in Bonn (all too safe). Quick work by the embassy there got the passports to London in time to prevent any minor embarrassment. Bonn's alacrity enabled me to conceal the gaffe from my boss — which somehow seemed important. But I suspect Mr. Pearson had some inkling because in his bantering way he asked me a few times in London whether I had the passports in safekeeping and his eyes twinkled at my slightly flushed assurances. He liked to tease. During lunch on the banks of the Rhine before the meetings, he announced mischievously that he intended to appoint as the next High Commissioner in London a prominent but very unlikely Canadian tycoon. I was sure, therefore, that he had already told a senior official present, who ardently wanted the job, that it was to be his after the imminent elections. He did not get the job in the end because the government was defeated at the polls.

During that campaign of May-June 1957 I did odd jobs for Léger especially as the Minister's office was concentrating on party politics which excluded me. When Pearson returned after the Liberals' failed national campaign, he thanked me warmly for the work I had been doing in his office. I protested that I had done nothing. There had been nothing to do in his absence. "Well, you did better than we did!"

Prime Minister Diefenbaker arrived a few days later and kept the External Affairs portfolio for himself temporarily. His office was awash with administrative and procedural problems as a small staff unversed in power struggled with an avalanche of paper and public pressure. The party had been out of power for twenty-two years. So much to learn after so much time. The Prime Minister's office was down the hall from mine and I knew his senior assistant well. He had been a colleague in External. Since Léger was on leave and my other duties negligible I offered to lend my pen to answering the high wave of letters crashing around their ears. The letters were literally stacked in tottering piles on the ante-room floor. I was awarded one pile. I recall letters from Native chiefs, senators and would-be senators, and friends and admirers of would-be senators. I sent suitably warm and non-committal replies signed by the Prime Minister or on his behalf. Just as my zeal for the intellectual content of such correspondence was beginning to wane, the quintessential letter arrived. It was from a young wife in the U.S. who had hung on her kitchen wall the picture of

Diefenbaker which had appeared on the cover of *Time*. Her young child sitting in her kiddy chair had previously "made strange" at mealtimes but now gurgled and cooed and swallowed her pablum as she gazed at the noble features of Canada's Prime Minister. I replied politely for the Prime Minister but sent copies of this correspondence to a senior colleague and the personnel chief, noting how my time was now spent. A transfer to the UN division arrived soon after.

One senior colleague in the East Block at that time was John Watkins, former ambassador in Moscow, whose superb knowledge of Russian music and the arts enabled him to provide Ottawa with a spectrum of insights garnered from cultural sources hardly tapped before by Western diplomats. John had taught a class of Chaucer I attended at the University of Manitoba just after the war. He seemed much the same in Ottawa, gentle and charming, but a little melancholy and bothered by ill health. He was an expert in Nordic languages and ended his career as ambassador in Copenhagen. He died of a heart attack a few years later after allegations that he had been blackmailed by the Soviets into spying for them. I am sure this was untrue. I do not believe he could have endured such a role.

These Ottawa years had results much more important to me than the East Block capers. A colleague invited me to a party to meet a dazzling Scandinavian woman. I was briefly dazzled but more seriously attracted by my host's sister, Nina Stone. She had characteristically adorned and structured her long hair with two knitting needles. She was a product of Ottawa and Edmonton schools, and a Queen's graduate. There she had been a rebel with many causes pursued through the *Queen's Journal*. Her summer jobs to flesh out a lean purse went from slinging plates at Moe's Place to, a more deadly task, writing obituaries for the *Kingston Whig-Standard*. Soon her sensitive and lively, musical and extrovert persona craved a wider field. Thanks to her father's generosity and her versatile handle on jobs, she financed two years in London, dotted with trips to the Celtic lands. She thrilled in Ireland, ancestral sod. She was a fill-in teacher in various murky parts of London and hit pay dirt with Thames and Hudson publishers. Back in Ottawa, she helped the Exhibition Commission prepare for the Brussels World Fair. Perhaps this prepared her for my own exhibitionism.

After a few months of visiting her rickety apartment off Rideau Street which housed a trio of spirited women, I clinched my proposal with a fruitless search in the basement storage room of my apartment for my mother's engagement ring before finally finding it behind the forks in my kitchen drawer. It thus began its second generation of essential service.

My parents-in-law were splendid people, both from farm lands pioneered by United Empire Loyalists in Leeds County north of Kingston. Ervin Stone was chosen to go to college, a rare opportunity in a farm family in the early years of this century. He went by boat on the Rideau Canal from Portland to Queen's. He studied medicine and spent his summers teaching Canadian natives in the west. This shaped his life. After medical service on the front lines in the Great War and directing a hospital in the U.K., for which he was awarded a CMG, (Companion of St. Michael and St. George) he became director of a mission hospital for native people in northern Manitoba, taking a growing family with him. By this time, the Canadian government was beginning to assume some responsibility for the health of natives and Dr. Stone was called to Ottawa, becoming one of the architects of a national medical service for native people and embarking on a career of struggle and frustration. After World War II, when he was once again in the army, he returned to civilian medical service, this time as director of the Charles Camsell Hospital in Edmonton, and administrative officer for Alberta and the Northwest Territories. After civil service retirement, he took to the sea as a cruise ship's doctor in the Caribbean. When this closed down, he found a different ambulation in Canada: he and his wife lived on a medical car up and down the railway lines tending the health of Canadian National Railway workers. They retired finally to a house in Forfar, not far from where Dr. Stone was born.

Nina's mother, Nellie, was a former school teacher whose one-room school had been near her village of Athens. At the end of World War I, she had travelled alone to England to join her fiancé, Ervin. He was looking after Canadian disabled in the hospital at Witley, Surrey, where they were married. She had a gentle art of persuasion, an almost Welsh gift of indirection, and defences in depth which were invisible but steel strong. She had a quiet sense of humour and a shrewd unshockability. She needed all her strengths and gifts to raise six children, one of whom died at sixteen years old, to get through World War II with three sons and a husband on active duty and to support Ervin in his difficult career. Nina's brothers tolerated me. Three were also in the foreign service, two ending as ambassadors. One made money in the oil business, not deigning to put his feet in "the public trough." The Stone family operated on mutual respect and affection.

On the subject of social drinking, however, their paths lay far apart. The offspring respected the view of the parents, strict but not censoriously teetotal, and brought no spirituous or fermented liquids home. All of them drank heartily elsewhere. As I was in a sense a star attraction, the only son-in-law, it was decided that I was an exception to Prohibition at Forfar. I kept a bottle of whisky in the kitchen cupboard and served myself the odd drink or two before dinner on visits. I drank alone.

At our wedding I acted as supply agent for Dr. Stone who wished to serve champagne at the reception despite his own abstention. All went well except that the local guests in this dry belt thought the "champers" was ginger-ale and knocked it back, leaving hardly enough for the Ottawa guests who had come a long way in a blizzard. Wedding speeches over, Nina and I left on posting to Malaya in this famous blizzard, entraining in Ottawa for New York to take ship for England.

The way to Malaya was the best part and all honeymoon. The first day on the Atlantic aboard the Queen Elizabeth, an elderly eccentric English couple joined our table. They were travelling under assumed names because on their last trip they had created what Cunard considered bad press. The United Kingdom tabloids had shown them in the ship's kennel sleeping each night of the voyage beside their beloved hound. Faced with six months' quarantine for him in England their affection rebelled and they had returned to New York City. Now they were heading back again incognito, confined to their cabin at night. Love of England and steep New York prices on a retirement income had overcome their tender hearts. The dog slept alone and quarantine loomed again. The wife predicted that Nina's bright eyes would "shine all over Malaya," and they did.

The trip from the United Kingdom by train to Genoa and by ship to Singapore was more energetic with stops and excursions. Taking a night off from the Suez Canal at the old Shepheard's Hotel in Cairo, we were served stale chicken sandwiches at 2:30 A.M. by a waiter in white tie and tails. Next morning during a claustrophobic crawl into the innards of a great pyramid we had to deal with a whimpering European ambassador afflicted by suffocation neurosis. Nina, who herself suffers from vertigo, still calls it her most disagreeable experience.

On our way out on the ship my inherited skill at deck tennis — my father had a low cunning technique — earned me only a tie for champion. On the way back from Malaya I invited my fellow finalist to a friendly drink or two before lunch. The match was set for 3:00 P.M. At that hour I rapped him up from a heavy snooze in his cabin. He was a corpulent English merchant from Hong Kong now rendered sluggish. I mowed him down. I still have the prize, a handsome silver frame. Or was that first prize in the fancy dress contest? I was fitted out as a shipwreck survivor dressed in long woolly underwear bottoms (in case of cross posting) and a life jacket decorated with seaweed (kitchen greens) from which hung various clipped-on useful objects such as lingerie and whisky bottles. The crew were said to be displeased by this gratuitous tempting of the storm gods. But we arrived safely.

Malaya (now Malaysia) was dull in cast and countryside compared to my first posting in India. But Malaya was host to a decaying terrorist emergency stoked by the Chinese government and drawing on an element of that community which had borne the sharp edge of the Japanese occupation. We went up to Kuala Lumpur (KL) behind an armoured train. The country was divided into secure and insecure areas with the latter still in the majority and vulnerable to communist terrorist attentions. This all faded fast when we were there. Meanwhile you broke the law largely enforced by United Kingdom troops if you secreted even a sandwich or a typewriter ribbon in your car going from KL to a beach town sixty miles away.

We opened the office in KL with the first High Commissioner, Arthur Menzies, young for the job but well-rounded in every way. He was a man of considerable experience with shrewd and well-balanced judgement. He could see swiftly through tangled complications. His easy sense of humour helped harmony in our team. His Asian background with boyhood in China and Japan was an asset in Malaya. Sheila Menzies was a helpful friend to us. Arthur went on to be head of mission in Australia, NATO, and

*With daughter Katherine, David, as Acting High Commissioner, dressed to attend the opening
of the first post-independence Malayan parliament, 1959, Kuala Lumpur.*

then China, a remarkably sensible assignment. During our postings in
Jamaica and Zambia the Menzies stayed with us. This gave us a felicitous
chance to entertain our Chinese colleagues who were genial in both cases.
The Chinese tongue flowed.

At our office also was a charming old administrative officer of the pipe-
sucking school, John Donald, who looked more distinguished than either
Arthur or I, and was sometimes mistaken for the High Commissioner.
Kuala Lumpur was still rife with U.K. merchants and residual civil servants
of the colonial era. Independence was only seven months back. A new post
in a new country should have been thrilling, but it was not. The leftover
U.K. officials were unenthusiastic about our aid overtures, perhaps a whiff
of national interest. We eventually had a million dollars to dispense according to the tortuous aid rules. "Menzies's Million" I called it. Luckily its
namesake was a sizzling pro at bureaucratic methods and handled much
of the aid work himself. He let me do most of the modest number of eco-
nomic/political dispatches we deemed worthy of emission.

By agreeable chance the British Foreign Office had posted my old
Cambridge friend Percy Cradock to Malaya a few months before we were
to arrive. He had cabled us to the ship at Suez, urging us to take a suitable

house he had chanced upon available for six months' temporary occupation. In the cascade of new embassies into a new country, suitable houses were as scarce as feasible office space. Our own High Commission had to squeeze into a few rooms in the Federal Hotel before we found workable quarters in a new building. Meanwhile, the Reeces were comfortable in Cradock's lucky discovery.

Our posting had two star turns, Prime Minister Diefenbaker and Katherine Reece. The latter came first. She was born almost literally under a palm tree in the simple cottage hospital called Bungsar in Kuala Lumpur. I was having tea at the time in the office I shared with the office stationery supplies in the Federal Hotel. Nina was more productively occupied. Perhaps because of tropical heat pressure-cooking her brain cells, Katherine later became a formidable scholar.

The second star turn was Prime Minister Diefenbaker. During his state visit in 1958 he was regaled with a lavish state dinner hosted by Tunku Abdul Rahman, the Malay leader and prime minister. At the request of the Tunku's speech writer, an Irish Muslim, we obtained approval in advance of the Diefenbaker arrival of a ten-minute speech text which we passed on to the hosts. When my boss, the High Commissioner, picked up Mr. Diefenbaker at the state guesthouse, the Prime Minister said, "Arthur, did you write this speech?" Lying frontally — as he later admitted to the real author, myself — Arthur said, "Yes." "Here," said Diefenbaker "you take it — it's better than most of the junk they write for me," and thrust the text into Arthur's startled hands. The Prime Minister then gave a 40-minute speech which bore no resemblance to my text but did draw on some of our briefing notes for his official talks. Forearmed with the discarded version, the radio interpreters for the three other Malayan languages were thrown into disarray. Irritated letters also appeared in the Tamil, Malay, and Chinese newspapers asking why they had carried extracts from the Diefenbaker speech which bore no relation to the actual speech they had heard in English on the radio. The speech began with pure corn. "Canada and Malaya will be friends until the snow falls in Malaya and the rubber trees grow in Canada." The diners were delighted. I have since quoted this passage in after-dinner speeches as a rare flower of egregious wit.

Mr. Diefenbaker's visit to Kuala Lumpur was piquant also for a new departure in gift giving. The event was suddenly moved forward in the program at the hosts' request. The protocol officer in our Prime Minister's party rushed into our room in the guesthouse and grabbed one of the gift parcels. At the relaxed little ceremony over a drink the Malayan Prime Minister presented "Dief" with an assortment of lavish local gifts. The Prime Minister proudly handed over his package. It was a large and ornate silver frame. The Tunku turned it over appreciatively — and again—and again. But there was no picture, no Diefenbaker in eagle pose. The portrait was face inward in the frame. The genial Malayans laughed with delight. As often with such major snafus, Diefenbaker laughed even louder. But minor snags often produced thunder.

The final item of the intensive program was a large buffet dinner on our lawn for Malayans and all the Canadian party, except the Prime Minister who was resting before the next leg of his trip. The food was highly spiced but a bit slender, Malay spiced meat on sticks called sati and a bit of salad. The results were rollicking as the liquid intake much exceeded the solid. One Malayan couple had to get us to move a car blocking theirs with a Canadian guest asleep at the wheel. When the Prime Minister's brother Elmer sensibly tried to go home, he was firmly rebuffed by a ragged but loud chorus of "Elmer's Tune," then a bright golden oldie. My ankle was almost shattered when I played goal in a dimly lit game of leftover ice chunk football. My assailant was a former Oxford Blue in soccer in the Prime Minister's party. Late night passers-by of the State Guest House were subsequently enchanted to see Canadian officials swinging hilariously on the nearby children's swings led, it was said, by the Prime Minister's mature and dignified private secretary.

A personal visitor in our second year was Roy MacLaren, an External Affairs friend posted in Saigon. Roy is a man of many talents. He has become an author, publisher, Member of Parliament, and Cabinet Minister. His visit to KL was just in time to help us shift from temporary bungalow number two to a long-leased house, perched beside a ravine and a retired rubber estate. While I kept the office wheels turning, Roy turned mover and helped Nina and our servants pack, cart, and unpack, trailing baby Katherine. Not much of a holiday.

We were also accredited to Burma from KL, but one week was my

Rangoon, 1958.

ration. I went with Arthur the first time partly because we assumed his accreditation ceremony would require at least two players. In KL three had been needed in an intricate ritual of bowing to the Paramount Ruler, and backing and filling performed with a hangover we had acquired in an irreverent and shambling rehearsal on our patio the night before. But Rangoon was different. Arthur was summoned to come alone at 10:00 A.M. to the Presidential Palace. Two hours later the President appeared apologizing for the delay. There was no ceremony. Arthur passed over his letter and stayed for a chat.

Rangoon was equally informal, in fact tatterdemalion. Ancient swollen American cars sauntered and chuffed through the streets, not interfering with the football (soccer) games played at the main intersections in the evenings and weekends. The Burmese were proud that British colonialism had dented their culture very little. Soccer and cutting the top-knot, a form of high-placed pig-tail, were said to be the extent of cultural penetration apart from the English language, still a needed tool in a land of many minorities. Rangoon at night was garish, noisy, and weirdly enchanting. Once imperial highways, the main streets now had wide strips of effervescent bazaar down the middle — the longest bazaar in the east! Walking through at night, I was offered every form of sinful gratification from small sisters to little boys. Resistance was easy.

Arthur and I pursued aid leads. There was already a modicum of Canadian technical assistance. We also visited the Commonwealth War Cemetery at a lush and peaceful spot called Insein. It was pronounced as you would describe those who were responsible for war's obscenities in such a calm and lovely countryside. Peace was still only fragmentary with large areas occupied by various insurgent groups including sizeable tribal minorities. This tragic and persistent situation was naturally a major theme in the dispatches I wrote on my return to KL after talking to Burmese, foreign diplomats and journalists. These were the first ever Canadian diplomatic reports on Burma.

Opening a new post meant that personnel departures had to be phased out and I was scheduled to leave before Arthur. I was posted to our embassy in Bonn. Nina and I decided to hit the seas again for the trip back to Europe, sensing that this might be our last ship chance. Inexperienced parents, we counted on our baby to remain in arms for the voyage. Hours, it seemed, after departure, Katherine took her first unsteady steps on the swaying deck. Happily, at Bombay, she attracted the eye of an Indian couple travelling with their trusted family servant who eagerly lent a hand. Our Indian friend turned out to be a bouncing Maharajah with a taste for cornucopia entertaining. He beat me easily in the ping-pong semi-finals despite a brush with mortality the night before. As usual he had gathered congenial passengers for a late night party, this time beside the pool. Abrim with champagne, he went down the kiddies' chute standing up. Like the man who fell from the skyscraper, it was "fine so far," until the back of his head hit the chute. He sank to the bottom and stayed there. An ironic death was only averted by the purser who was quietly monitoring the affair. He jumped in and hauled out the brawny ruler. So the Indian state was not headless — only swathed in bandages.

CHAPTER EIGHT

Bonn and London
(1959-62)

BONN WAS A short, sour fragment. It began prophetically when we were met at the airport by the embassy's number two man in his Mercedes. By smart embassy footwork our own new car, a more modest product, was also waiting for us at the airport. My family safely in his car, I followed my colleague into town. But after twenty minutes I realized I was following the wrong grey Mercedes. Alone in a strange town with little German, it looked like a long afternoon. Luckily I did know four words in German: yes, no, left, and right. After several false trails these brought me to the hotel where Nina and Katherine had long since been installed.

This lost leader beginning was a foretaste. After I had finished a few weeks of language school I learned that my mother in London had inoperable cancer with only a few months to live. My former boss in India, now the boss in Bonn, helped me to get a transfer to London. My mother eventually died in our house in Chelsea. On the many occasions since when I have been angry with the personnel gentry in External, my righteousness has been softened a shade by memories of that humane transfer. The department was small enough then to permit such civilities.

The short time we had in Bonn was dogged by lack of a house and by ill health. I spent Christmas of 1959 in bed in our hotel with a rumbling appendix. At the local clinic, however, they told me that these abdominal attacks, which had bothered me every few weeks for three years, were actually caused by diverticulitis. But they kept coming, somewhat alleviated by ice packs to the gut. One day in Ottawa about four or five years later the ice pack did not work and I found myself enroute to the operating theatre in the Civic Hospital waving my Bonn X-rays and diagnosis in medical German, as the elevator doors closed around my pleas about diverticulitis. The appendix was removed in the story-book nick of time. I also had diverticulitis, in fact, but a type which did not cause much pain.

I was sorry to leave Bonn because my colleagues there were congenial. I invited one of them to have lunch with me for a discussion of our assignments and the local scene. She was a little surprised when, in a last minute economy measure, I took her home to lunch instead of to a restaurant. Home was a cramped temporary apartment lent to us by the Australian Embassy. Fresh minted laundry mingled with the reek of peppered sausage and cabbage rolls. Katherine and her diapers were visible and audible. Lunch was tasty but very plain. Our guest was polite but probably unattracted by this raw slice of young domesticity. Fortunately it did not deter her from a subsequent triple career of marriage, children, and professional work.

Our departure from Bonn for London in March 1960 echoed our arrival. Just as we headed for the door on our trip by car to the Channel ferry, bags in hand and apartment spotless, Katherine anticipated the Channel by vomiting in a wide arc over the living room rug. Bonn riddance!

Not many junior First Secretaries in London, home to about a hundred and fifty embassies, have a frontal encounter with the British Foreign Secretary. I did — and enjoyed it. In 1961 our High Commissioner, George Drew, was on holiday. I was desk officer for Asia and the Middle East in our office. Britain and the Soviet Union were co-chairmen of the 1954 Geneva Conference with continuing responsibilities for the International Commissions in Indo-China of which Canada was a member. Canada and the U.K. held different views on an important issue. Disappointed that this disagreement had not been discussed in the corridors of a recent NATO ministerial meeting, I decided, without instructions and with a cool nerve, that we should tackle Lord Home, the Foreign Secretary, on the subject without delay. Our amiable Chargé agreed to my brash resolve and we made our way into the cavernous and hideous Foreign Office.

Accompanied by a junior minister and a sardonic senior official, Lord Home outlined the U.K. view with trenchant conviction. Since the Chargé was new and I the resident expert of a few months standing, I laid out the Canadian view — less effectively than the Foreign Secretary since it was a weaker case. After a last look around the vast office — I swear that mist clung to some Holbeinesque paintings on a distant wall — we made our escape. I must admit that, subconsciously at least, the aim of my escapade had been to get British views at this high level across to Ottawa because these views were right. A few weeks later Canada accepted the U.K. position, with significant consequences in deterring the spread of conflict. Flexibility, ability to see the other side of the fence, a shade of ambivalence are sometimes useful in furthering the longer-term and wider interests of one's country.

Much of the work done by the High Commission was concerned with trade, economic and political relations, as well as military liaison and cultural affairs, and the busy river of consular and immigration matters. My own duties were to tap, filter, and shape into reports U.K. political and economic information, as well as views on Asia and the Middle East. Since colonial days and then Dominion status, Britain had given us considerable access to valuable sources of information and analysis from their wide network of diplomatic posts. They still did. This cooperation was, of course, tinged with some self-interest and aimed at influencing our policies, but we profited more on balance. My field of responsibility was for areas where we had few posts. The eruption of the Congo (now Zaire) after independence in 1960 fed our impetus toward new posts in Africa. My colleague who covered Africa was on leave at the height of the Congo convolutions which meant a lively and fascinating summer period for me.

Thus I trotted daily, sometimes twice a day, across the Mall and along the Horse Guards side of St. James's Park to my usual source, the Foreign Office, skirting 10 Downing Street. Then back to dictate hopefully succinct but often long and detailed telegrams. By dint of practice I could do these by the yard in final form, a knack which served well in later posts.

A mellow source of pleasure in London was the Reform Club. Scorning the Traveller's Club which was stuffed with diplomats and Foreign Office chaps, I joined the Reform which was almost adjacent. Thus I could lunch my Foreign Office contacts, my main point in having a club, at a handy establishment other than their own. Although Talleyrand had slid down the Traveller's bannister, the Reform had served Liberal leaders since the Great Reform Bill. A photo in the Morning Room, the main assembly point for browsers and drinkers, showed a phalanx of Liberal hierarchs arrayed in the Morning Room with the same furniture but in the late evening of the nineteenth century. Lord Rosebery, then Prime Minister, headed this gathering. The club had since then severed its link with the party and its membership is non-political although many Liberals do belong. But so do many Treasury officials. Diplomats could join without fear of accusations about domestic political interference. I did so with the aid of an old Cambridge friend — a barrister of right-wing leftish politics — the Reform attracted such if only because of its name. And so I spent many filigreed hours in the club beneath its high-ceilinged gloom, reminiscent of a cleaned-up railway station.

The Reform was a focus of literary and academic London as well as progressive politicians one glimpsed in the "cold room" (i.e., where a buffet lunch was served). The Morning Room was the scene of my brush with the literary heights. I was there drinking coffee after lunch with two Canadian literary academics. We had been looking at Henry James letters in the club library. James lived in the club for a time. Suddenly one of my literate companions clutched my arm and stiffened with excitement in the approved manner. He pointed out an elderly man chuckling in high-pitched mischief to similar companions. I had never seen them before but I had a hunch that my companion's excitement was on target. I checked quietly with the hall porter. "Yes, Mr. Forster is in to-day." For my friends — and myself — seeing E.M. Forster was like an old-time bobby soxer seeing Frank Sinatra. We hung on his words and chuckles while pretending our own conversation. My lunch was a *succès fou!*

Another use of the club gave me a sophisticated but childish pleasure. I would sometimes drop in before lunch straight from the Foreign Office awash with their subtle views and judgements on some neuralgic spot.

These I would decant in outline onto club writing paper, feeling as I did that Lord Palmerston might have sat there a century before jotting notes for a barbed speech in the House.

During one pleasant session in the club, lunch with a senior Foreign Office official, we quietly swallowed two bottles of red wine after two pink gins. This was double the usual intake. The wine was French but the talk Algerian. I was told of a newly-minted Foreign Office belief that, despite his public posture, President de Gaulle had decided to get rid of Algeria. Aglow with this important and prescient assessment as well as the lunch lubricant, I hurried back to Canada House five minutes away by foot and dictated a fairly lucid and certainly important telegram to Ottawa. Once this historic message was delivered to the Comcentre I relaxed. In fact, I was almost asleep when a thin, bright, sprightly figure marched into my office. It was Howard Green, then External Affairs Minister, on an official visit to London. We had never met before but I knew that he was a strict teetotaller. He sniffed the vinous air of my office and asked me if I was an administrative officer — presumably one addicted to English pubs. I wanted to explain my momentous lunch and discovery but I could not think how to do so without stumbling over the pink gins and all that wine.

A more ebullient and much less austere Conservative politician was my boss in London: George Drew, former Premier of Ontario and Leader of the Opposition in Ottawa. When he saw me in the corridors of Canada House, he would sometimes call out, "How's Louse?," his own version of Laos of which he knew little. But once when I was away he handled a complicated negotiation with the Foreign Secretary concerning Laos with a trained lawyer's skill.

He was also sensitive and very kindly in staff relations. When my mother died he phoned me at once to offer the services of his executive assistant, an officer one rank higher than mine, to help with the funeral arrangements. For a small private funeral at a crematorium this was not necessary, but he himself attended it.

Drew spent much of his own time on the economic side of our work and was a hot and sometimes indiscreet opponent of Britain's entry into the European Economic Community (EEC), a bid that failed at the time. This dislike of a major U.K. policy fuelled Drew's dislike of some British ministers whom he illustrated pungently at some of our weekly cabinet meetings — as we called our staff gatherings which the chairman invested with a more portentous flavour. Once he asked me to represent him at the airport the next morning and provided me through his assistant with a plausible excuse for not meeting a Canadian cabinet minister who was simply changing planes in London. That night Drew came to a cocktail party at our house. It was a lively affair with some liquidity. As he and I rolled down the stairs sometime later, he gave me an entirely different excuse to use next day. Naturally I planned to use the latest version. But next day with throbbing pain between the eyes damned if I could remember which excuse was which. It did not seem to matter. But when I met the Minister and passed on the better sounding excuse, he alarmed me by insisting that he phone Drew from the VIP lounge. After their chat the Minister gave me a very dirty look. Clearly I had used the wrong excuse.

Although Drew's views and tactics on the Common Market issue were controversial, his judgement proved impeccable on the apocalyptic crisis of our time — the Cuban missile confrontation. I can testify. Because of the threatening stages of the Cuban crisis, Nina and I were trying to decide whether she should accompany me to a meeting in Paris and leave Katherine behind in London as planned, or take her with us, or cancel Nina's holiday. Trying to be realistic in the very real shadow of nuclear death, we were leaning toward annihilation togetherness. On Sunday, October 28, 1962, I was in my office preparing for the Paris meeting when I ran into Drew and told him of our dilemma. He replied with vigorous confidence that the crisis would be over in a few hours. The Russians would stand down. And they did — two hours later. A unique send-off to Paris; full marks to George Drew.

Although less prescient than Drew, I had in fact been working on Cuba for a few days as the crisis swelled. I was theoretically responsible for reporting U.K. views on Latin America. We had by then adequate Canadian coverage in this area through our own embassies *in situ*, so only once did I step into this field. On Monday, October 22 we had received a high priority telegram from Ottawa telling us to find out urgently if the Americans had asked the U.K. to suspend landing rights for Soviet and Eastern European flights en route to Cuba. Washington had just asked Canada to do this. Clearly a crisis in Cuba was imminent. The senior Foreign Office official we saw had no word of such a request to the U.K. or of U.S. intentions on Cuba. But his big boss had. Long afterwards I learned that President Kennedy had phoned Prime Minister Macmillan the day before our call on the Foreign Office to brief him on U.S. plans to force the removal of Soviet missiles in Cuba. I assume this secret word on high had not yet reached the Foreign Office when I first saw them. I kept in touch with the Foreign Office for the next few days but the harvest was thin. British handling of the crisis stayed at the highest political level while middle levels were confined to speculation and acute concern.

We had a full social diary in London. We fed into our official parties friends from our two separate London pasts. The leavening was good although it was sometimes hard to tell which was the lump. (Certainly not one Australian whose husband eventually became ambassador to Washington. In one set of small hours we invented a new form of dancing to records — we danced on top of them.)

Our friends from the different streams naturally did not know each other. One injudicious mix edged nastily to confrontation between a German couple, old friends of Nina's, and a burly barrister from my Cambridge days. He was in full ebullience, puffed with wine and a clear dislike of Germans from war experience. Hasty verbal footwork by the hosts averted raw conflict. I found that our German friend, plump and amiable, could also prickle when tested. I did so on a different occasion. West Berlin was then under strong Soviet bloc political pressure. Annoyed by his unfair criticism of NATO, I cruelly referred to the need for a Final Solution for Berlin. He was angry with me and, I suspect, the past.

Our ample barrister friend had mortal luck. He died of a stroke while young. Perhaps his barrel girth saved me from a like end. After a lively dinner in our Chelsea house I found that he had gone home in my suit coat, leaving behind his own tent-wide garment. That such a switch was physically possible was a strong impetus to diet.

Another old acquaintance from Cambridge helped to turn our social wheels. This one was a rugged Welshman, Russell Lewis, who had become a Tory party official in London. As a neutral diplomat I decided that it would balance the bias of my political youth to attend the Bow Group Ball with him. The Group were serious younger Conservative thinkers. Their night of frivolity was pretty dull but the aftermath was a long haul to daylight in our house with much amber fluid and bonhomie. Nina finally went to bed leaving me with the surviving guest, Lewis. This called for a sustaining breakfast and I cooked up some tough but tasty liver and kidneys which he chewed up with pleasure before I drove him to his flat in Wimpole Street, a rather risky journey with Katherine bounding around the back seat and my head bounding in tandem. The next day — much later the same day — I was told with acidity that not only did I look like the dog's breakfast but I had also eaten it. The resemblance to human vittles had been uncanny — in the whisky dawn.

A star turn of our modestly swinging social style in London was a young Canadian musician called Galt McDermott who was the son of a senior External Affairs official. Galt played the piano in pubs while composing popular music. We were complimented when he and his wife came to dinner with us once or twice, thus missing a hatful of quids in the "local." He played *chez nous* after dinner — you could not have stopped him. On a soupy summer night his cheerful sound through the open windows caught the ear of a young policeman. He came to our door to enjoy not arrest. This gave a giggling woman guest a child's dream fulfillment. She snaffled his helmet and ran up the stairs wearing it. The helmet was passed from head to head while the complaisant owner refused to ruffle — until he mentioned his fiancée in Kenya and Nina asked if she was black. Emphatically not. He left tersely but the piano sang on through the night.

The pianist moved on from pubs to Broadway where he composed *Hair* and the like before the sixties were out. When we arrived in New York on posting in the late months of the decade we decided, perhaps stupidly, that we lacked the gall to look up this famous figure on the basis of a slight acquaintance years before. But he might in fact have enjoyed a chuckle about the music-loving bobby. After all he had liked our dinner well enough to pay for it, in effect, and play for it too.

Our house, furnished by the landlord with pleasant copies of antique classic furniture, was an upbeat feature of our London life. (In those days you had to find your own housing. External now saves money by buying or long-leasing houses which are provided to embassy staff in return for a rent share extracted from their allowances, and those of official Residence occupants.) Our London house was a block from King's Road, artery of Chelsea, near cinemas, smart shops, Chinese restaurants a long way from home, heaped-up antique stores, and pubs galore belching with business. In those days call girls were legally permitted to advertise discreetly. One ornate antique shop of expensive quality carried a notice in its window in sharp contrast to the other goods on display — "Dusky Lola says hello," and a nearby phone number.

Two near neighbours, Dick and Ann Romyn, claimed to be among the few surviving artists in expensive Chelsea. They had bought cheaply and restored a studio house at the end of our street athwart a wine warehouse which blocked through access. The Romyns became fast friends. For us they opened doors to creative London through their many talented fellow artists. Nina and Ann with their little girls spent many happy hours in London's great parks and museums. In one of his large oils featuring fishermen of vaguely Indian aspect, Katherine, then about four, is pointing an elegant foot for, we hope, posterity. We bought a score and more of Romyn oils, drawings, and other works which remained a warmly valued part of our cultural baggage in post after post. Although well-rated on the art market now, our Romyns will never leave our caravan. The Romyns were a truly continental melange — Swedish/Dutch/British/Jewish.

A neighbour across the street was of tall English elegance. We called her "Lofty." In the London manner we did not know any part of her real name. She was the cause of mild perturbation one hot summer afternoon. Two seedy-looking men of no fixed purpose appeared on our street and sniffed around. Romyn hung out of his studio window comfortably stripped to the waist when a large Rolls-Royce drew up accompanied by a police car. Dick had been thinking of calling the police himself to report the two shady characters. It was not necessary. The Queen had come to tea with her friend "Lofty."

The King's Road was the scene of a sad milestone for me. For the first time young men (i.e., younger men) began to slide past me with ease as I trudged to the tube station at my maximum and sturdy pace.

Normally my duties in London did not include consular work but like most other officers, I had to take turns on the duty roster after hours. This caused me to scramble one evening when a rather tremulous old man phoned me to say that the airline would not let him on the homeward flight to Montreal because his Canadian passport had just expired. The airline could not be persuaded so I rushed to our office in Trafalgar Square and found some sort of stamp — unconnected to passports but looking official and impressive — and scrawled over it in my inscrutable handwriting that the passport was renewed for a week. The old man flew home with thanks.

A serious and tragic consular case involved a widow on our doorstep. Her husband had just died on a railway platform in London. They had not booked a hotel room in the city which was stuffed with tourists. The hospital phoned me. It was Saturday night and I was duty officer. Pouring myself a stiff drink, I sent Nina to fetch her. We had a spare room. The widow was a considerate and charming guest. Despite shock and grief she was selfless enough to worry about bothering us. Mercifully we had rye whisky in stock. It was her only tipple. With medicinal aims we persuaded her to drink deep and Nina tucked her into bed. Before then she had explained that she and her husband had been attending Dieppe raid anniversary ceremonies. Her first husband had been killed there. Her second husband had fought there. She thought the strain of the event and journey had been too much for her husband's heart. The battle had thus cost her both husbands.

The next day she was again anxious not to disturb us but three-year-old Katherine entertained her and Nina took her to Covent Garden market to see the flowers. She was a florist by profession. I spent that Sunday trying to cut through UK mortuary red tape to enable her husband's body to accompany her on the charter flight to Canada that night. But there was no relevant pathologist on duty and the only one I could trace with the help of the Home Office was staying in a country pub outside London. He had just gone off on a day's tramp across the North Downs. Without an autopsy the body could not go with her for no extra charge on the charter flight. I had the sad residual duty next day of arranging for its shipment at high expense on a regular flight.

Our London posting ended in December 1962 and we were due for a home assignment. This time it was indeed our last journey by ship. The many diplomatic journeys that lay ahead were all by air. As the boat train for Southampton pulled out of London in the early morning, a crippling fog rolled up the track. It proved to be the last killer fog in London's history. Clean air acts ended this romantic but deadly staple of London life.

CHAPTER NINE

Ottawa and India Again

(1963-69)

WHEN THE WHITE régime in Rhodesia chose to defy Mother Britain in November 1965, I was head of the African section of External Affairs in Ottawa. The purpose of the Unilateral Declaration of Independence of November 11 was to delay indefinitely the evolution of full parliamentary democracy in Rhodesia, named after the great Imperialist. With one man one vote, power would have gone to the large black majority, where it now resides in modern Zimbabwe. We in Ottawa persuaded our masters to cut all trade ties with the rebel colony, as requested by Britain, a year ahead of the eventual mandatory United Nations sanctions. The crisis led to the first Commonwealth Heads of Government Meeting held outside London. It took place in Lagos at the invitation of the courtly Nigerian Prime Minister, Sir Abubakar Balewa. It was concerned solely with Rhodesia for three intensive days in January 1966.

The meetings and all the delegations were comfortably enfolded in the bosom of the huge Federal Palace Hotel. We met, ate, and slept there. In fact, I saw nothing else of Lagos except the turbulent road to the airport and, come to think of it, the Bagatelle and Kakadoo nightclubs where we helped entertain the gallant secretaries after their long stints of overtime. In the Federal Palace Hotel, Dr. Hastings Banda, leader of the Malawi government since their independence, wore his famous homburg, one of the symbols of his leadership, from his hotel room to the conference rooms three floors down. No rain fell.

Mr. Pearson, then Prime Minister and feeling liberated from domestic political roiling and scandals for this sunny interval in Lagos, played a strong role. The conference adopted two resolutions he put forward. One, which I believe was born in my Ottawa bathtub, established a Commonwealth committee to monitor the effects of sanctions. This helped avert the departure from the Commonwealth of some African countries angered over the lack of military action against Rhodesia. The second measure favoured by us and also advocated by the first Secretary General of the Commonwealth, Canada's Arnold Smith, was designed to coordinate and stimulate aid to Zambia which was damaged by sanctions against Rhodesia while highly approving them. Throwing new bodies into the pot succeeded, as often, in reducing the heat. Much heat and thunder had been put into the conference initially and understandably by the African leaders with the burly Prime Minister Margai of Sierra Leone taking the lead. A solid object, a committee, or some other chunk of machinery can act as a common denominator which bridges acrimony. Britain's Harold Wilson rode out the storm with beguiling eloquence which impressed and somewhat amused our Prime Minister. He told us that if you listened to Wilson for very long, you could well believe that the Rhodesian régime was about to crumble into dust. An acceptable compromise outcome to the conference was fostered by our own delegation's solid work which was powered as much by our concern about a split in the Commonwealth and an exodus of African members, as it was by sympathy over the British dilemma.

My own role was mainly to churn out speech material which Mr. Pearson drew on in summary form during the informal ebb and flow of discussions in the conference. I chipped in rather too frequently during meetings of the delegations and those of our small knot of ambassadors in Africa who had been convened in Lagos to brief our Prime Minister on African views. These sessions were enlivened by Pearsonian anecdotes of high level shenanigans as he relaxed in congenially confidential surroundings. He had the last chuckle on my blatherings at the meetings. I told him that I had known Singapore Prime Minister Lee Kuan Yew at Cambridge where he was called Harry. Since I had not had a chance to talk to Lee in Lagos,

Pearson was perhaps growing sceptical of my claim of old acquaintance-ship. So he asked Lee and came back to report with a smile that "Lee remembers you well as a thin, quiet chap!" I was neither any more.

The conference had a deeply sad aftermath. The same day he saw Pearson off at Lagos airport, Sir Abubakar was killed in a coup against his government. Since he had been fond of the dignified Nigerian leader, our Prime Minister kept us wearily busy the weekend of our return in briefing him on developments in Nigeria, where a new military government had taken power.

The Rhodesian crisis added weight to our case for more Canadian posts in Africa. The persistent efforts of Tom Carter, director of the African and Middle East Division, helped to escalate our pathetic total of two or three missions in black Africa into a dozen within a very few years. This was con-sonant with the burgeoning numbers and importance of independent African countries. The crisis also helped to stimulate more official African visits to Ottawa. On one occasion when neither Carter nor I were available to host a lunch for a visiting African Minister of Justice, I asked Allan Gotlieb to fill in for us. He was then head or acting head of our Legal Division and firmly on the fast track escalator to the top jobs in the depart-ment. He accepted cordially but phoned back the next day asking to add a guest to the lunch, one Michael Pitfield, then a fairly junior officer in the Privy Council Office. I knew Pitfield slightly and two of his attractive sis-ters somewhat better. I had first seen him as a small boy eating corn on the cob in 1945. Perhaps influenced by this image, I told Gotlieb that Pitfield was far too insignificant to be included in the lunch for a visiting cabinet minister. Thus with my usual prescience I annoyed not only a future head of External Affairs, but also the future king of the civil service and sword arm of a long-reigning Prime Minister.

I spent four years in Ottawa during this period, 1963-67, the first two as head of the Middle East section and then two as head of the African sec-tion. My Middle East work was not remarkable except for an Israeli diplo-mat's informal complaint that we were too determined to be rigidly bal-anced in our policy for the area. Not true. My three principal mentors during this assignment were Arnold Smith, Ralph Collins, and Tom Carter. Smith moved out in 1965 to ten impressive years as the first Secretary

General of the Commonwealth. He successfully built up this role in the
face of what I believe were attempts by U.K. officials to preserve British
predominant interests and influence in the Commonwealth. His reports
previously as ambassador in Moscow were legendary for length and
insight.

Ralph Collins replaced Smith as Assistant Under-Secretary after being
head of the African and Middle East Division and ambassador in South
Africa. Ralph was an impeccable headquarters man with a crystal mind. He
was a good boss. He left me and Carter alone much of the time, stepping
in when required with subtle but incisive authority. We maintained a common interest in football beyond this period together in Ottawa. When I
returned from Ghana in 1976 and found that Ralph's health would not let
him walk very far, a Ghanaian solution was found. I felt sure that the
Ghanaian High Commissioner and his son, my son's age, would enjoy a
look at one of our cherished tribal rites. His Excellency was amenable and
the five of us were chauffeured right up to the grandstand in his Cadillac,
flag flying and all barriers down. We did this twice. I suspect the first time
was curiosity and the second pure courtesy. It was getting cold for
Ghanaians — and for thin-blooded Canadians fresh from the tropics.

Tom Carter was my immediate boss for three years as head of division.
His balanced judgement and cheerful energy were given full play in the
southern African arena, especially when the Rhodesian crisis unrolled.
When Tom and I were colleagues again in Vienna a decade later, I gave him
a farewell lunch. In my toast to him I could not resist mentioning that Tom
had pursued measures against the illegal régime with such vigour that
I was at work in my office for two months non-stop, no weekends, no
holidays, no days off. It was true and in a good cause. Tom protested that
he had been no office tyrant. And he was not, but he certainly took his
work seriously.

A trip to Paris during this period for an international meeting brought
me near to a literary genius. Sodden from a driving rain which had as usual
swallowed up all the Paris taxis, I was the last dinner guest to arrive at our
NATO ambassador's residence. And the only one without a dinner jacket.
My host had assured me that black tie was not de rigueur. I felt damply
loutish but luck seemed at hand when I sat down at a table next to a

Katherine, Caroline and Michael with nursemaid Mary Masalimani in the Reece house, New Delhi, 1967.

Michael in India, 1968.

Mrs. Cameron. Aha, I recalled that my host was an old friend of Elizabeth Bowen and I dimly remembered that she had married someone with a name like Cameron. Besides, she looked like the face on the back of Penguin books. It was indeed she. I told her that, just before my present trip, I had taken one of her books out of the library for my wife. An agreeable coincidence. "Oh," said Bowen, "which book?" Damned if I could remember in the crunch the name of any of her books, although I had read three or four. Thoroughly abashed, I did not try to engage her in conversation again. In any case, her table mate on the other side was the Belgian ambassador to NATO who was a resistance hero, littérateur, and charming raconteur.

Nina needed library books. Although she had time to create a parents' group to rate local television programs for children, she was largely housebound for two good reasons: Michael and Caroline. Our two youngest, bouncing blondes, were born in Ottawa during this home posting. Michael almost did not make it up the long steep and icy hill to the Civic Hospital in January 1964 while Caroline arrived with verve in the late autumn of 1966. Our brunette, Katherine, began a long immersion in French with enthusiasm. To our pleased surprise there was a small and good French school in our next post, New Delhi. Caroline made the long air journey to India in 1967 as a squeaking nine-month-old, while Michael turned in a rave performance of his own, charming a ring of grannies as a non-stop world traveller of three and a half. He had tearfully watched his toy horse disappear into the moving van on our lawn in Ottawa. He raced up and down as horsey came out of the crates in New Delhi. He ran to get a pail of water for the bullocks pulling the mover's cart.

My second posting in this horrible and endearing land began in July 1967. Our three fellow travellers, junior division, were instantly and warmly engulfed by the south Indian *ayah,* Mary, whose husband John led the four indoor servants. John was particularly attached to Michael whom he named Bombay Express for charging around the large reception rooms before hiding behind the curtains to chew on forbidden fare. Caroline, known simply as "Baby," staggered around with zeal and shared Mary's curried food in preference to her own imported baby foods. These were given away to an orphanage. As elsewhere, Nina orchestrated a complex household and conducted our entertaining from duos to full symphonic buffets for fifty. She also served on the executive of the Delhi Commonwealth Women's Club (known to the husbands as the Delhi common women), playing a hands-on charity role. She took courses in Indian politics at the university and taught music at the local nursery school where Michael picked up a flashy brand of Hindi.

Capital News Photos, New Delhi.

Nina and David greeting the Indian President in New Delhi in 1967. High Commissioner
James George is standing behind the President.

This stay in India was made the more interesting because of my first posting there ending ten years before. The Indian economy had burgeoned by comparison. The Green Revolution had been imported with swift almost dramatic effects on grain productivity as a result of the new techniques. Severe droughts which had slowed down these gains temporarily were over before my return. Indian industry, with some roots in powerful dynasties such as the Tata and Birla families, had developed rapidly with foreign cooperation. Inherent Indian scientific, engineering, and economic talents, plus an ancient bazaar skill of shrewd merchandising, were instruments of change in a traditional society.

Population pressure remained an overriding and almost overwhelming problem. The Indian population in the late 1950s was estimated to be about 370 million. Ten years later it was 700 million. Spasmodic and sometimes drastic control methods were not working.

Soon after we settled into our spacious but architecturally rather cold house, we set off for Calcutta, capital city of the state of West Bengal. Gross misuse of resources or not, Canada was staging a film festival in Calcutta as part of our centenary celebrations and we had to represent the new High Commissioner James George who had just arrived in New Delhi. In Calcutta we did see something of Mother Teresa's city, its squalor and its filth and misery. But our path lay mainly in marble halls. We lunched with the Governor and his Swiss daughter-in-law. The voluminous setting was the former Viceroy's palace built by Lord Cornwallis after he lost the American colonies at Yorktown in 1783. This vast building must have been a consolation prize.

Indian state governors were roughly equivalent to Canadian lieutenant governors but with potentially more power. The present incumbent, linear descendant of Cornwallis, was a tough little Indian civil servant who had been tutored and tempered under the Raj. He was soon to take over direct rule of the state by fiat of Mrs. Gandhi's central government. He replaced the elected chief minister who had led a shaky coalition including communists of two flavours, socialists, and dissident Congress politicians like himself. During our stay in Calcutta, the chief minister was still precariously hanging onto office. He received me sitting behind his large half-moon desk piled at every curve with soggy looking files. Wearily he asked me if we had Communist parties in Canada. I well understood the reason for this enquiry: Bengal Marxists were the main thorns in the side of his shaky government and the reason for its imminent collapse.

I am sure that the governor enjoyed providing the smack of firm government. He was a crisp but pleasant lunch host. Rumbling began overhead as we sat in the centre of a vast dining room. Nina asked the question I hesitated to put. "Oh," was the reply, "those are my grandchildren roller skating in the ballroom." Sic transit Raj.

We met another form of entertainment at our hotel, the *gharao*. This labour weapon was simple. Instead of walking off the job, you locked management in. You confined them to small hot rooms surrounded by striking workers. These stifling little dungeons often produced quick settlements. It seemed unlikely to happen in our case because the *gharao* against the hotel management had to be focussed on the whole building instead of one hot spot. A fierce and sloganeering crowd surrounded the hotel but

Nina (far left) and David (far right) at a fancy dress party in New Delhi, 1968.

within its management were enjoying self-contained, air-conditioned comfort. They may have lost some guests. We found it a very edgy experience to walk through a tough crowd of loudly chanting Calcuttans with truckloads of police in shields and batons lined up across the road.

At the centennial film show, the audience, such as it was, was more decorous. The required police permit had not been received until two days before. Since the local film society, acting for us, could not advertise or inform their members until the permit arrived, we had only half a house. And they all chose to sit in the gallery which they knew to be the best viewpoint. Thus, the tiny governor and I had to peer and project upwards our jewelled words of introduction. Then we scrambled up to the gallery to see "Helicopter Canada" and other good National Film Board productions. While not addressing Calcutta's harrowing problems, they may have entertained and enlightened a little some of the people tackling these problems.

Culture was not high on my plate as number two in the High Commission, although I did supervise the two second secretaries who worked on public and consular affairs. In addition to such overseer chores, a major staple of my work was to be chief reporter, drafter, and editor of political and economic telegrams, and letters to Ottawa. This meant regular séances with senior gurus of the Indian Foreign Office. It also required a more extensive reading of the several verbose English language newspapers than my appetite had room for. One senior official I enjoyed talking to — or, more accurately, being talked to by — was an old Cambridge college mate, Jagat Mehta. By coincidence he and another St. John's College undergraduate friend, Percy Cradock, had both been the objects of violent crowd hatred in Peking during the Cultural Revolution (which provided an ironic echo in reverse of Goering's dictum that when he heard the word culture he reached for his revolver).

I talked to Mehta and others often about China. India had maintained relations through war and vilification while we had no embassy or diplomatic ties, and hence no direct source of contact or assessment. I felt myself to be a part-time officer in a phantom Peking embassy. Indo-China took the biggest single slice of my time, however, as it had in London six and seven years before. I was thus a semi-pro — at least in my own eyes. This time there was an even more direct and shared interest. Canada and India were both members of the International Commissions in the three countries with Poland the third member. India chaired. My usual Indian dialogue mate, K.C. Nair, was a senior Foreign Office hand from south India. He was a courteous and pleasant interlocuteur. This was a help because Indian and Canadian views were not exactly on all fours all the time. Bitter clashes often soured the meetings *in situ* of the commissions. In Delhi I had general instructions to keep in frequent touch with the Indians, and specific instructions on Indo-China Commission problems were often cabled to our office from Ottawa. Mr. Nair's smooth style and simpatico persona took the rough edges off some neuralgic policy disagreements. Matters were also helped by a free flow of cashew nuts and tea whenever I called. (At my farewell dinner for Nair I noted in my toast to him that I had only one complaint against him — but this was a very serious one. He had fattened me up with cashew nuts.)

My instructions for these tea and nuts sessions naturally reflected Canadian views influenced by the United States position, while the Indians were distinctly influenced by the Soviet Union. But our exchanges in Delhi became heated only once — when I passed on verbatim some tough comments from Ottawa. My usual method was to paraphrase, reshape, and edit, not to soften the core but to make the surface more agreeable and hence more likely to have some positive effect. I never again departed from that practice in discussions with Nair. I think he and I did some good work. We helped to sustain enough mutual tolerance and agreement, or at least acquiescence, to keep the commissions viable. They still had at that time a stabilizing and deterrent influence — the latter in a very small way — in a situation of long-term collapse.

Another damaging side wind from East-West tensions affected our task in Delhi. We had been watching and reporting India's tortured reactions to the Soviet tanks in Prague in the autumn of 1968. India's human rights inheritance and parliamentary democracy clashed with Soviet aid and influence. In the middle of an autumn long weekend I was phoned at home by a nervous young duty officer. I was then in charge of our office because Jim George was on a northern trip. The entire Immigration section was also out of town. A great time to be told there were twenty or more Czech families in our rather scruffy office seeking immediate entry to Canada.

My first instinct was to tell the Czechs to quit India immediately and we would process them en route for immigration/refugee status in Canada. Then I recalled they could not get on a plane without income tax clearances. Our bilateral relations with India also counselled informing the government rather than sneaking the Czechs out. Ottawa and George on his return agreed. The Indians were at first warmly cooperative. Then police guards surrounded the Czechs in their hotel. Soviet influence was at work. After a few days of havering amid countervailing pressures, including their own concern for human rights, the Indians issued the necessary clearances for all the Czechs concerned after their embassy had exercised the normal right to speak to them. Meanwhile one refugee family had been turned back at the airport for lack of the needed papers and Jim George persuaded another couple at the door of his residence not to seek asylum there since this might have upset the whole applecart.

Our relief at the exit of this group of Czechs was only mildly diluted by comment in major Indian newspapers that Canada had deliberately lured these skilled metallurgists, etc. away from a very useful Soviet aid project in India because such mining skills were in global short supply. I asked the Ministry of Foreign Affairs official concerned, whom I knew well, to issue a corrective statement or at least stimulate an accurate version in the press. He promised to do so. Nothing appeared and we decided not to print our own statement for fear of appearing to protest too much. The undoubted Indian government role in the press stories did not really surprise or annoy us. Apart from the damage to a valuable aid project, hostility to and from Pakistan was a continuing reason for Indian concern to guard and nurture its relations with the Soviet Union despite Indian instincts, education, and institutions akin to the West. Indian action in letting the Czechs go was thus a brave step in the raw East-West situation after the Soviet tanks had brought winter to the "Czech spring." A slanted press story was small atonement.

In 1968 Nina and I joined Jim George at a ceremony dedicating a high dam in Kerala, the far south-west state. Canada had provided much aid to this project. We had breakfast at a state government bungalow with the chief minister and the energy minister of Kerala, both Communists. But they were of different wings, one lefter than the other. They exchanged greetings over the fruit but we were told afterwards that they had not spoken to each other for months because of policy differences. This must have made for grumpy cabinet meetings. Nothing like generous western capitalists to bring the leftist boys together again. Neither leader could have been enraptured by one feature of the main inaugural procedure, pouring the first concrete. As a bow to deep custom the Kerala leaders had acquiesced in a religious kickoff for the ceremony. Brahmin priests chanted and prayed at the propitious moment they had chosen for an event dominated by communist speeches. India, land of bizarre overlaps.

James George was a brilliant and unusual man. His strong philosophical bent found full scope in Eastern religions. He and I were not soul brothers but the old cliché about opposites attracting helped us to team up usefully. I respected his intellect. He appreciated my desire to get on with things.

Nepal was the only dual accreditation from India. Nina and I had one trip there, in 1968. I did my business at the foreign ministry and talked to colleagues in the three resident embassies to pick up the flavour. This still left time to see the fascinating and exotic temples, palaces, and markets in

Kathmandu and the nearby small town of Pagan, a crafts centre. Above all, in every sense, were the Himalayas. On a superbly clear day we took a special tourist flight which circled near Everest as the passengers bobbed up and down to photograph this majesty. Not satisfied yet, we hired a taxi to take us to see the sun rising in a spectacular dawn panorama over the peaks. The road trek began in winter darkness and cold in the well-weathered taxi. In the dim light the road looked and felt like the craters of the moon. We jounced over and around giant potholes for more than two hours. We reached the top of a ridge just in time to see the sun's first rays delicately touch and then transform like an electric charge the incredible chain of the Himalayas. Top of the world was not a cliché. "Never did sun more beautifully steep in his first splendour valley, rock, and hill ...." Never did Wordsworth sound so flat.

On the return, we walked as much as we could and not just to shorten the lurching taxi torture. "Bliss was it in that dawn to be alive." The air was crystal, the countryside magical, and the villages out of a medieval scene from Oz — realm of the Good Witch of Nepal.

Apart from a brief but vivid bout of "mountain fever" during a hill station holiday, we and the younger children survived the multiple health hazards of India. These included the krait, a swiftly lethal snake which killed a gardener in the nearby Soviet compound. Katherine, like many foreigners, just did not take to Indian conditions and was stick thin. She had amoebic dysentery which can be fatal. No pediatrician or specialist diagnosed the cause of her persistent, general poor health until her appendix flared up in the middle of a Delhi summer night. The emergency operation was complicated by allergy to the anaesthetic and an overdose of antidote. She was so weak her chin lay on her neck and we feared for her survival. Because of, or in spite of, our sending for doctors in all directions, demanding intravenous feeding and engaging a private nurse, she was soon out of danger.

Our regret at passing up a chance to spend a third year in India was firmly mitigated by relief at getting the children, especially Katherine, to a healthier climate. We decided to take our final leave in India in the hill station of Gulmarg, high above the June heat of the Vale of Kashmir. With our *ayah* Mary, who had never flown before, we took a plane for Srinagar and then took taxis to the end of the paved road. From there Gulmarg was approached by pony track which wound through the pine forest. This meant a sharp encounter with the local horse *wallahs*, all of whom wanted our custom. Michael was practically pulled apart at the arms in the good-enough natured tussle and I had to Solomonize the situation before turning to the problem of getting Mary into a saddle. She had never ridden a horse and weighed around two hundred pounds. With a *wallah* lifting on each side she bowed down a sturdy beast and I got my money's worth.

A few days later we rode and then walked up the nearest mountain with Katherine, leaving the others with Mary back at Nedou's hotel. After some time and a steep rocky climb, I agreed to stay behind with Katherine while Nina chugged on up to take some photographs down into the next valley. I had been up there twelve years before. For some reason our guide did not go on with Nina; I expect he did not quite understand what was happening. When he began to get nervous and talk about crevasses, storms, and danger, I started to get worried. The British High Commissioner came trekking down, noting that Nina was up there alone in the mist, and eyeing me censoriously. At last she came into view, having slid down a glacier on her heavy mountain boots behind some Japanese trekkers. She had indeed come to rest by a rock and encountered a lurking crevasse big enough to fall into. A mountain lesson for all. A final Kashmir memory of Caroline swinging back and forth on the stately balcony of our wooden hut which was a pageant of old fretwork and carved roofs where eagles gathered in the first bright dawn and took the sun. We flew back to Delhi in a plane lurching through a sand storm.

CHAPTER TEN

New York and Quebec
(1969-72)

IN 1969 WE moved from New Delhi to New York in early autumn. My title in New York was impressive, Minister and Deputy Permanent Representative of Canada to the United Nations. But the job proved less so. The UN, especially the General Assembly, seemed to be often a round of labour-intensive blather conducted by self-important delegates who lacked touch with reality. In their committee rooms beside the East River they seemed to think they were making history by passing resolutions which had no bite and no legally-binding effect except for the occasional Security Council resolution which escaped the veto and fell within a narrow band of enforcement. Perhaps I over-reacted to my first exposure to multi-lateral diplomacy but my views today of the UN then are not much different. Mercifully, times have now picked up. With the end of the Cold War, the veto is in virtual disuse. The UN, led by the Security Council, is now taking firm action towards international security. This seems to be having a bracing effect on the General Assembly.

The UN in 1970 was labouring over the wording of its twenty-fifth anniversary Declaration. Unanimity seemed out of reach. Our delegation was largely responsible for the final achievement of a unanimous document but the rest of the world took little notice. A committee had laboured on the Declaration and the anniversary arrangements for months. I was

pitchforked into play late in the day when failure loomed, largely through
gaps in acceptable wording between Third World countries and the
Western powers, especially those with residual and former colonies. South
Africa and Middle East issues were also deeply divisive. In October I went
to a routine reception in the UN dining room where they made appropriately sprightly Manhattans. I had two or three. Fearless, I went to my
evening meeting of the twenty-fifth anniversary committee. Its deadline
was imminent. I put forward some fine-spun compromises — or so I
thought them. They flopped, especially with the colonial powers.

The next day, Saturday, I walked through crisp autumn to Bloomingdale's
upper- middle-class emporium to buy a pair of gloves. On the way back,
chewing sourly over the previous night and my strike out, I began to think
of the six or seven major gaps in the agreed wording of the Declaration
draft. Perked up by smart new gloves and the tang of autumn air and gas
fumes, I worked out some quite subtle but simple wording to stitch over
the residual holes in the garment. Being wiser for my experience of the
night before, these compromise words were more in the centre than my
previous formulae. After further refinement on the Sunday I showed the
proposed amendments next day to our office expert who was mildly
approving. My wholehearted ambassador was enthusiastic. Ottawa agreed.
That night I had to give a dinner for visiting parliamentary observers,
Members of Parliament from Ottawa. I thus missed the plenary session
which was the last chance to complete the Declaration before the anniversary day. After robust advocacy of our amendments by our ambassador,
Yvon Beaulne, they were accepted and the Declaration was unanimous.

After triumph, fizzle. The full text appeared in the New York Times but
received trifling attention in the rest of the international media. I had earlier been teased about floridity by a colleague for proclaiming in the
Assembly that "we must not present the world with a vacuum." I doubt if
the world would have noticed. The UN failed in 1985 to produce a forti-
eth anniversary Declaration. This caused only minor ripples. But no one
can take away from me my Bloomingdale amendments. And the gloves fitted well.

One reason for my general unhappiness with my diurnal role in New
York was that I was to be in charge of the delegation's economic work, a

field which was not my forte. I discovered the change in the Minister's assignment shortly before leaving New Delhi. My predecessor's role had been on the political and general side. As a masterpiece of the genre, I commend the telegram I received from some personnel snake in Ottawa before I accepted the posting. I read, "The duties of the position are too well known to require description." How to fit square pegs, etc., without actually lying. Worse still was the custom of sending people from Ottawa to fill the top jobs on economic committees in New York. So I could not get the experience to become the expert I did not want to be.

I got a bit luckier in my second year. The Member of Parliament from Ottawa who was supposed to be the delegate on a political committee of the General Assembly wisely realized, I suspect, after one visit, that there was not much future in it for him. He never came back and has done very well since. I became the *de facto* delegate and was able to combine intellectual interest with frustration.

As often happens *en poste*, colleagues make an important difference to the rewards of the job. In New York, Ambassador Yvon Beaulne as a stimulating boss made this difference for me. His generously emotional temperament kept us all going through the arid stretches. He led our attacks on verbal excess with tact and skill. His success among his UN colleagues drew on his rich bicultural Canadian background, his leadership qualities, and linguistic prowess also in Spanish and Portuguese.

Godfrey Hearne was the third man in the office, the senior counsellor. He was a highly intelligent and subtle man with a sharp sense of humour. He worked mainly with Beaulne but I took pleasure in his company, not least when he gave me a lift home. Hearne succeeded me as Minister in New York. The last time I saw him we were having cardiograms in the Ottawa Health Centre en route to our respective postings in Thailand and Ghana. The cardiogram did not help him. He died tragically of a heart attack in Bangkok.

The summer of 1970 the Reeces drained their pockets and rented a large house at Bayville on Long Island where the family escaped the sweatbox New York heat, stress and pavements, and I used up my yearly leave. Most of the summer I tackled the fabled Long Island Railway to Oyster Bay and dreamed of F. Scott Fitzgerald. At rush hours it was sweat at close quarters with rocks occasionally shattering the windows as we passed through the murkier passages on our way out of New York's sprawling ugliness. When Beaulne was on leave, I would be met by the ambassador's limousine and chauffeur as I emerged from the elbowing multitudes. Meanwhile at Bayville the landlord's crabby Alsatian guarded our kids, preventing anyone else from going into the local library when they were inside.

Adopting the New York apartment dwellers' ritual, we took a winter cottage for weekends for the rest of our posting. The cottage was near the gross wooden summer houses in Southampton, summer palaces eerily empty in winter, with sapping waves beating at their foundations as we walked against the Atlantic wind. After work on Friday we took the Long Island Expressway through the great tunnel, naming all tunnels thereafter "dragon's teeth" (for the lights in their ceilings).

Being a family of five (plus a temperamental *ayah* brought from India), in a twelfth storey apartment even on the elegant East Side presented one of our greatest "cultural shocks" in a career of many. I was able to walk the forty blocks to work, zigzagging to avoid red lights. Weekends by the ocean, great schools, including the French lycée for Katherine and Michael, galleries, theatres and music, and the unique New York zappy flavour almost made up for the drawbacks of big city living. But not for the uncongenial job. My vocal unhappiness with my role at the delegation helped to stimulate an offer from Ottawa to spend the next year in Quebec as members of the federal government's bilingualism and biculturalism program. We jumped at it.

My work experience at the UN ended on a rising note. At the 1969 Assembly our External Affairs minister, Mitchell Sharp, described the UN, with some accuracy, as "drowning in a sea of words." It was then suggested to us by fellow delegations that we should back up this assertion with action or forever shut up. In 1970 we obtained Assembly approval to set up a committee to consider changes in the rules of procedure to cut down the time-wasting and gaseous oratory. We thought a committee of fifteen members would be businesslike while covering the spectrum of regional groupings. The Yugoslavs, however, thought in bigger terms. They did not fit into the Eastern Europe group. They calculated that the smallest committee they could get on to was thirty-one members. Guess who would be thirty-first? Their very able ambassador, who later rose to political heights at home, was looking for a new arena in the off season. After considerable ambassadorial acrimony we had to accept the wider net because several extra delegations wanted in.

After initial high suspicion that this was a device to amend the Charter and scrap the veto, the Soviets and their friends eventually abstained. A vote against would have had a possibly crippling influence on our project. By chance I had a hand in nudging the Russians into abstention. When I was chargé in the summer before the resolution was launched, I was regally summoned by Jacob Malik, the Soviet ambassador, who was also deputy foreign minister with long UN experience. In debate he could be very tough, ranging to brutal. After I explained to him our very modest ambition of procedural reform, he was not fully converted, as witness the eventual abstention, but he seemed more relaxed about our initiative and became positively amiable. He even went down with me in the elevator of the Russian building, a great courtesy to a mere chargé, but the Soviet minion running the elevator sent us up first instead of down. Malik bristled with irritation. I suspect he dumped on the wretched minion as soon as I left.

After the 1970 Assembly, the "Committee of 31" was put in motion. I was usually our delegate and, thus stimulated, concocted forty-eight ways to improve the rules of procedure, not all of them enchanting to staid cautious Ottawa. I had to leave before the work was finished but some good changes were made — even in my absence — despite the obstruction of those delegations who like oratory for its own sake and those who had an overgrown bump of protocol (e.g., those who liked to see proceedings and work suspended in all seven committees and the plenary for the whole day when a VIP died). At the death of de Gaulle funerary tributes replaced business eight times over. It does not happen now. My last speech at the UN was in the Committee of 31, assuring the Soviets once more that we did not aim to amend the Charter.

Despite this rather positive ending I felt a lift of the heart as we drove through the unlovely streets of New York past the Bronx and over the Hudson en route home in 1971. We would miss Lincoln Center and our illegal parking place beside it, Central Park and both the Mets (opera and museum), but an unsatisfying job in a city of raw crowded ugliness made two years quite long enough.

Quebec City was not a foreign capital, but after nineteen years in the foreign service it was our first posting in a non-English language except for that brief stretch in Bonn. The bilingualism program we joined consisted of twenty federal civil servants from various departments with their families spending a year in Quebec City. We were scattered around the suburb of Ste. Foy in leased houses. Our aim was two-pronged; to "perfect" or learn French as spoken in Canada and to learn Quebec. Both prongs worked. We had a six-segment program: the government language school, Laval University courses in subjects of our choice including French as a second language, official trips en masse to all sectors of the province, part-time work with the provincial government, three current affairs seminars a week in French, and excursions and special occasions in Quebec City environs conducted by members of the Laval faculty.

The Laval Extension Department under the courtly Abbé Greco organized all our programs. We played a hand in arranging and chairing the seminars and were able to attract a gamut of politicians, journalists, business executives, and academics. This was 1971-72, only a year after the October crisis, the murder of a provincial minister and kidnapping of a British diplomat in Montreal which severely shook Ottawa as well as Quebec. We thus had lots to talk about. For some reason we had only a thin turnout from the Quebec government but a full range of Parti Quebécois (PQ) leaders.

One prominent PQ leader was the speaker during a week when I was chairing our seminars. It thus fell to me to refute his patronising suggestion that he speak to our group in English — "Otherwise no one would understand me adequately." He then tried a second tack. He would at least have the question period in English since complex and technical economic subjects would be too much for the audience in French. Again a sternly negative response from the chairman, thankful that the year was sufficiently advanced that the group's French would be too.

After the question period in stalwart French I gave the speaker a lift to his hotel. I asked his views on a likely scenario of events if Quebec decided on independence one day. He asserted without a sliver of hesitation that

Prime Minister Trudeau would use the federal army to stop this. I strongly disagreed. I am sure also that no Trudeau successor would use force to try to keep Quebec in Canada. Examples such as Yugoslavia's civil bloodshed must surely provide a deterrent.

My work for the provincial government was in the sub-ministry of the Environment where I mainly translated documents. Oral French practice was provided by an amiable federalist in my office who lunched with me. More practice was gained by my rather presumptuous appearance as guest lecturer on Canadian foreign policy at the Université de Québec in Rimouski. The students were doubtless amazed at my anglo accent and shaky grammar, but it was a case of not what the dog said but the fact he could speak at all. Nina sat at the back and recorded my errors of syntax. Afterwards we gave dinner to two of the professors concerned. I mentioned the likelihood of a posting that summer as an ambassador. Seeing concern on their faces, I hastened to add that it would be in an anglophone country.

Nina and I were educated in Quebec to features we had not grasped in odd weekends in Montreal over the years. Coming directly from the U.S.A. and particularly the vast metropolis of New York with its teeming millions of more or less anglophones, we were strongly struck by the incredible achievement of this very small North American minority of francophones. They had preserved their language and culture for centuries despite enormous pressure from the English language all around them. At the same time we noted the effects of such influence at the mass level. The Quebekers were more American in surface and popular ways than Ontarians. This included clothing, pop music, love of baseball, holidays in Florida and New England. There were family ties with the "Canucks" of New England whose ancestors had emigrated there in waves during hard times in nineteenth century Quebec. In the harsh winter of Quebec City we remembered the courage of the early settlers.

My conviction was reinforced that French can survive better in a bilingual federal state structure than it could on its own. Canada provides a form of buffer state for Quebec. Alone in the anglo sea, Quebec would find American culture storming through the doors and windows.

Our children adjusted well. Fortified by two early years in the New York French lycée, Michael plunged into eight weeks of *unilingue* summer camp and then grade three of the local francophone public school. He swam well. After a few months he noted to me in front of an amused Laval professor, "Katherine, she's *bilingue* but me — I'm a French." Katherine had an easier haul. After eight years of studying all subjects in French in three lycées in three countries she jumped two grades into the venerable and much respected convent in Quebec of *les Ursulines*. A tribute to the lycée system and especially to the prime quality of the Manhattan branch. Caroline, without any prior exposure but aided by her clear untrammelled mind in a paucity of years, passed via a bilingual nursery school into eager chat with the neighbour kids. *En famille* was indeed a valuable plus. The Quebec program sadly ended a few years later, apparently for lack of support by federal government departments.

Bilingualism had been a farce when I joined the service in 1952. You had to testify in applying for entry that you had a working knowledge of your second Canadian language. In most cases this was fiction. My French was better than that of a lot of fellow recruits but it was *quasi* abysmal. No test, no tuition, no tangible incentives were provided. My francophone colleagues learned English fast. They had to. Almost no French was used in the federal government at that time. A respected ambassador of Quebec origin, who retired early after being ambassador in Cairo, told me that his farewell report was the first he had written in French. The option had always been there but he had clearly not used it because the readership and impact would have been slender. He then became Agent General for Quebec in Paris.

Two solitudes and one language. This has changed sharply in the federal government. Much credit belongs to Prime Minister Pearson for the initial shove and for policy guidelines. English still gets majority use and more, but the proportion of French used has grown both in written and spoken dimensions. The practice now is to catch them tender. By the time of my retirement, young foreign service recruits did not go out on their first posting until they were adequately bilingual, taking months of non-stop immersion, if necessary. This makes excellent sense. The linguistic balance should swing further away from English dominance as the younger officers move up the ranks.

A friend from Montreal wrote me a letter when we were having a brief romance in my bachelor days in Ottawa. She apologized for its cool tone. It was written in English which was, for her, the language of business while French was the language of the heart.

In July 1972 I was made High Commissioner to Trinidad and Tobago, the major Commonwealth country in the Eastern Caribbean. Mr. Pearson asked me at a reception at the end of the Quebec year why on earth I was going off to a rock-girt anglophone bastion. I had to answer, "Because that's where they're sending me." Basically, the Quebec experience was designed to fit us to be bilingual representatives wherever we served. In fact, they were considering a posting to Cameroun for us when someone else was picked to go there. I found out later that, unknown to Cardinal Léger at his mission in Cameroun, External Affairs had decided that he would feel more at home in a French-Canadian foyer. Fair enough. And with all due and much respect to Pearson, the Trinidad posting fitted well into my past and future career pattern of Commonwealth developing countries, seven out of ten postings.

CHAPTER ELEVEN

Trinidad and Tobago and the Eastern Caribbean

(1972-74)

ANXIOUS TO MAKE a good impression on my first Prime Minister at the start of my first posting as ambassador/high commissioner, I recalled the parting shot of Lester Pearson when he told me with a wintry smile to give his "cold regards" to Dr. Williams, Prime Minister of Trinidad and Tobago. Somehow in the long journey south, this greeting warmed up. When I presented my credentials to Williams, the regards elicited a seemingly cordial grunt. Pearson knew best, however. I later learned from a Canadian banker that Williams told him there had once been a bitter row between the two Prime Ministers. So much for the two volumes of Pearson's memoirs I had bought out of my own pocket to give the Trinidadian leader.

Not that it made much difference. The crusty Dr. Williams distrusted the "metropolitan powers," among whom he included Canada. He did not have much time for their envoys — or any others. While we were there he announced his retirement but was persuaded by colleagues to think again. He easily beat his only opponent in the party leadership convention. However, he went into virtual retreat for the rest of my time there.

There were specific bilateral issues which annoyed Dr. Williams. Chief of these in my time was Canada's decision to drop a rebate on customs duty on Commonwealth Caribbean sugar which was in effect a subsidy on those exports. The exports had, however, much dwindled in volume. I suspect that we dropped the residual rebate for no better reason than untidiness in the eyes of our fiscal authorities. In any case, Dr. Williams was now all the more inclined to lump us in pejoratively with the United Kingdom and the United States as "metropolitan powers" even though we never had any colonies or gunboat diplomacy. In point of fact, it must be conceded that we did have the largest embassy in town because of substantial trade, aid, and immigration programs; the only time in my ten postings when we were the biggest boy on the block. Williams may have feared undue influence.

We got a much warmer reception from Dr. Williams' cabinet colleagues. One in particular considered that relations with Canada were important to cultivate. He was consistently friendly and helpful and we had a fruitful ongoing exchange of views within the confines of our national interests. On one occasion close and frank collaboration between us averted a situation created by Dr. Williams' unfounded suspicions which would have damaged both countries. He thought we were ganging up with a third country to injure Trinidad. In the process of averting a nasty squall I had to disobey directly an instruction to brief the minister orally on the true position but on no account to hand over a written text about the point in question. My friendly cabinet minister pointed out, however, that showing Williams the text was the only way to convince him. So I gave him a copy. The verboten text did the trick. The land mine was defused in Dr. Williams' mind, and Ottawa did not cane me for disobedience.

My eventual farewell call on Dr. Williams in 1974 was cordial in tone but insubstantial. A senior economic minister told me soon afterwards, however, about an important Trinidad initiative in Canada-Trinidad relations which had been passed to Ottawa by their High Commissioner there before I had seen Williams. I was thus able to provide our Department with some comments and avoid looking like an incompetent out in the cold. If you are dealing with a reclusive and unhelpful head of government, be sure to cultivate his ministers.

Our relations with the Prime Minister had perhaps not been advanced by an incident during a Canadian National Defence College (NDC) visit to Trinidad before my tour there. Dr. Williams was of various racial origins including African. When the NDC student concerned, known to his colleagues as "Minibrain," met the Prime Minister at a reception, he congratulated him on his tan. "I was born with it, you fool, " cried Dr. Williams, stomping away. Tough but not so gentle, he was held in high esteem and electoral value by his fellow islanders. We too had to admire the consistency of his crustiness, his intellectual calibre and integrity, his honesty, and his political skill in riding with one foot on the electoral corpus of each of the two main ethnic communities, African and East Indian. His reputed habit of turning off his hearing aid when faced with a bore, including ambassadors, was endearing. (He never did it to me — as far as I know!)

Prime Minister Williams directed a promising economy in Trinidad when I was there. Before the seventies, sugar had been the leading economic engine with tourism gaining ground. Carnival had helped the latter in Trinidad and the simple beauty and charm of Tobago was also an important magnet. Much of the sugar was grown by peasants of East Indian origin imported as estate labour. This is a basic factor of Trinidad politics. Since independence, its governments have reflected a slight black majority. The governments have been led by black prime ministers. There have been two unsuccessful attempted coups since independence, one with armed forces input. Parliamentary democracy proved its strength. Dr. Williams' successor was eventually defeated in free and fair elections, as was the successor's successor, A.R.M. Robinson.

Canada's economic aid program was starting to phase out before I left. Tourism and, more importantly, Trinidad's growing oil industry, especially offshore, were the main factors in a per capita income rising above that deemed eligible for development assistance. But oil raised our trade and investment prospects of mutual interest. These were facilitated by major Canadian banks on the islands. Alcan also had a facility in Trinidad for transferring bauxite to large ships for the trip to Canadian refineries. The bauxite first had to be transported downriver in smaller ships from the major extraction sites in Guyana. To develop our economic ties we had three young and eagerly capable trade officers in the High Commission who covered all the Eastern Caribbean islands.

Dr. Williams was not the only blunt Trinidadian. I had the pleasure of hearing the daughter of another senior Trinidadian put down, heavily and decisively, an ambassador's wife who was being too oily in her attentions.

The wife cooed that she had noticed during the recent Carnival extrava-
ganza that the Trinidadian father's eyes had lit up when a "certain person"
had danced across the stage in costume in a band of masqueraders. The
girl retorted tartly that she had in fact tripped and stumbled. "Oh, indeed,
the stage was rather rough and uneven," replied the diplomat's wife. "No,"
was the reply, "I was drunk." End of dialogue.

Carnival. Little need be said about this riot of long legs, gaudy costumes,
and compulsive steel bands bouncing endlessly down hot streets and
across the stadium stage. It has been described and pictured ad nauseam,
a condition some masqueraders end up in. Our first year was sedate. We
followed prescription and attended on the Sunday evening a contest and
display of costumes, extravagant and sometimes grotesque, of the Kings
and Queens of the Carnival, bands of masqueraders as well as steel bands
(pounding tintabulating oil cans — or stroking them). Calypso singers also
contested. Most of them were called "Mighty" something or other (e.g.,
"Mighty Sparrow").

After the competitions and crownings we had a modest carousal and in
the dawn of the Monday, known indelibly as "Jouvay Morning," local
patois for opening day, we sat with the Mayor of Port-of-Spain to judge
informal bands of masqueraders of limited means and home-made costumes. This was called "Ole Mass." These contestants were rich at least in
imagination. They specialized in sardonic portrayals of local VIPs (e.g., a
police officer who was then rounding up urban guerrillas wearing a duck-
shooting cap when out on the manhunt). Nina had failed to spike our coffee thinking we had had enough of spiked fluid. Thus our appreciation for
the spirited if ragged portrayals ebbed sharply as the sun rose.

The next year, 1974, we went for broke. With our seven house guests
after the Sunday night contests, we joined a British small hours party of
very high octane. After stiff gin-and-tonics for breakfast, we helped push
a steel band on its float through still throbbing streets. This was a traditional but boring thing to do. We had sent our driver off earlier and were
thinking of a taxi home when we ran into one of our house guests alone
on the street, the others having vanished in the convivial melée. He was in
fact our "outdoor" house guest, an overflow whom we had parked in
a nearby Chinese hotel but fed well chez nous. He was and is a brilliant

historian and was then head of an English university, eventually trading this in to preside over an Oxford college and serve his shift as Vice Chancellor of that ancient seat. Not, it would seem, the human stuff for what then unfolded (i.e., for playing "Ole Mass" in the pulsing dawn).

In fact our guest was game indeed. He was heading to England by the noon plane and bed was not on his mind. We hailed a taxi and asked the driver to wheel us to Independence Square. He instantly drove us instead to the nearby Seaman's Union where he obtained and sold to us at swollen price a large bottle of rum, just the right sequel to *petit déjeuner à la gin*. He then dropped us at the square where we were absorbed into a large band of masqueraders playing "Ole Mass" with jumped-up zest. They were all painted and sprayed with black and gold and we were so anointed. We joined the jump with souped-up esprit. This helped us to inhale the taxi rum with less damage than we deserved. We hoped eventually to dance with our new friends past the mayor on his reviewing stand where we had sat in semi-sober boredom the year before. But the crowd in the square was bulging. Movement forward, as opposed to up and down, was sluggish. Finally at about 9:00 A.M. I told Nina we would have to go home to avert a photo in the press the next day showing the Canadian High Commissioner lying in the gutter. She said, "You always want to go home too early!" — but allowed herself to be dragged across the square to a providential taxi. Our children and six indoor house guests were taken aback to find two black persons in our bed that morning. The other guest wrote to say he had scrubbed all the way across the Atlantic — but it was well worth it.

I did get into print after all two days later. Nina danced through the streets on the Shrove Tuesday playing straight, not "Ole Mass," in a large band of masqueraders. She was dressed as an undersea polyp. She appeared on the front page of the main newspaper the next day having a drink on the side of the road with a very tall beak-nosed Englishman, also in her band, during a break in the jump action. This picture was captioned, "Canadian High Commissioner Go Play Mas!" This caused great joy to our house guests but later that day I had a pensive phone call from the photo editor of the paper. "The Managing Editor say that picture don't look much like you." When he asked if I wanted a correction printed, I said, "Not on your life. Don't you print a word. It's the most popular thing I never did in

© Trinidad Guardian.

Nina dressed as an "undersea polyp" in a Carnival band of masqueraders February, 1974, in Port-of-Spain.

Charity Ball at the Canadian Residence in Port-of-Spain, New Year's Eve, 1973. Nina is at the right corner.

Trini." So all ended well, although we heard that the tall man's wife, who had been standing on the other side of him, was not much amused.

When a prominent member of the ruling party died we were invited to the funeral. We sat almost on top of the casket next to the Prime Minister. It was very hot and airless even though the church, like many in the Caribbean, had no glass in its large windows. Nina felt rather faint as two back-to-back sermons took us almost through a second hour of humidified lament. Luckily a crowd of, shall we say, less distinguished citizens were clustered outside the window. Suddenly a burly gent leaned through the window frame from outside and said in a loud voice of menace, "Das enuff, man, das enuff!" And it was. The second sermon ended swiftly. Hasty prayers and we were out in the breeze. A valuable example of infenestration.

Bars and bars. I was called to the Bar in England in January 1951. I had stopped at various other bars en route. This rendered my part in the proceedings rather loud and clumsy and visibly displeasing to my sponsor at this Inner Temple occasion, a senior judge. His aversion to my performance might have been softened if he had known the evening was a short break for me from the lengthy sorrow and pain of watching my father die in a London clinic at the age of 57. But what has this got to do with Trinidad? A friendly local lawyer persuaded the Chief Justice that I should be called to the Bar of Trinidad since I was a member of the sister and ex-mother Bar in London. It was made clear that I was becoming a regular, not an honorary member, and our office was later pestered by a worthy citizen who wanted advice about a legal problem involving goats. At the Call to the Trinidad Bar I was decked in a borrowed wig, presented by Attorney General Hudson-Phillips with eloquence, and received graciously by able, amiable Chief Justice Hiyatali. But I was not called on to reply. Custom forbade. I did hold forth later at a law-laden lunch at my Residence to a captive audience of luminaries. In Barbados custom was more genial and I replied to a charming address of welcome by Chief Justice Douglas. My first and last legal plea.

Why did I bother with this folderol? Public relations and increased access to an important element among the ruling élite. There was also a minor side benefit, a rather good joke by the eminent old English judge,

Lord Denning, to a legal gathering in Trini which I attended as a local barrister, *soi-disant*. I often used the joke later at after-dinner occasions. I was subsequently amused to hear from daughter Katherine in England that she had heard Lord Denning give a speech in some legal forum and he had used "Daddy's joke." Denning also came to Ghana when we were there but I missed hearing him and his joke. I mentioned to a congenial Ghanaian friend and lawyer that I had been amazed to see barristers in the Caribbean required to wear wigs in court. This was ridiculous in that sweaty climate and clearly a silly vestige of colonialism. "Well," he said, "we do too."

Our children were pleased with Trinidad. A big house and sloping garden above a golf course. The parents were much less happy about the garden until we had it snake-fenced in close-knit metal mesh. Because of its proximity to the South American mainland, Trinidad has very poisonous snakes. The worst was the coral, in two sizes, the smallest the deadliest. So our children kept their shoes on. But they loved the sea and surf which were forty minutes away over a cliff-curving and hill-climbing road. The surf was fun for all but another source of parental vigilance. The undertow could be deadly. We were more relaxed about the schools which were of reasonable standard although a reverse tongue transition was required from the French of Quebec. Children seem to swim through these changes easily but it is often tougher below the surface. Nina arranged French lessons for all the High Commission children.

Katherine found Trinidad English a shade baffling at first after ten years of lycée and Quebec French, but the school was an interesting mix. And she made three good friends who ranged the spectrum. One was the daughter of a doctor of mixed race, one the child of a judge of African descent, and one the child of a Jewish refugee family from Europe who owned a clothing factory. After one year, we decided it was time to settle Katherine in a high-calibre boarding school in Canada to top off her multi-country parade of schools. She went off with enthusiasm to Havergal in Toronto.

Security was not an overwhelming problem in our Trinidad Residence. We had a secure door on the staircase which was shut at night and also when we went out in the evening to protect the children. A police car swooshed around our driveway every few hours. Nothing ever happened except the arousal of our dog one night. We decided afterwards that his furious barking might have been aimed at a nocturnal friend of a resident maid who was friendly to visitors. After we had been on the island for some months, I was found to be on the hit list of young rebels mentioned elsewhere in this chapter. They included professional killers among the young idealists. So the police car came around more often.

Mixed luck with servants in Trini. Lucky to have any, I hear you cry, but diplomatic representation in a Canadian high profile area cannot be done in a large domestic plant bereft of helping hands. And the hands are not expensive in the Third World — and employment much needed. Of the three positions in the Residence only one was filled on our arrival and she was expected to leave soon. She did. Nina found a splendid large and handsome cook who was soon lost to marriage and maternity. We attended her wedding, an uneasy affair since the groom arrived forty minutes late — in cowboy boots. One maid was incompetent and fired herself before the axe fell. Her successor was a bright little thing but announced after a few weeks that she was pregnant and "he," her "baby father," did not want her to work any longer for fear of damaging his progeny. Marriage was not at issue.

Ill luck then dogged our servant situation. A pleasant new maid got mumps and wanted to convalesce in her mother's house sixty miles away. We sent her in our official car. Contrary to all our instructions, the driver loaded the car with relatives and then hit a molasses truck, killing one of the relatives and breaking our maid's jaw, a horrible insult to injury. The noon radio news reported that my official car had been wrecked on the highway with five deaths. I knew this was not the Reece family en masse because the car had been going to the maid's mother's house. Nina had not planned to go with them. The two younger kids were in school where I had dropped them that morning. But what if Katherine had decided at the last minute to see some countryside? So after a truly agonizing delay I got through to Nina and asked whether Katherine was around. She was. Then I was able to tell Nina about the news report. As I spoke to her, I spotted our thoroughly wrecked car parked in a yard by the dockside across from my window. Our office was swamped all day with anxious phone calls about the ride we did not take.

Eventually we found a good and mature cook but she thought our house guests too numerous (so did we) and our local guests too strenuous. At last we hired a jewel and paragon of a servant but soon had to pass her on to our successors. All in all, in two years we had nine servants in the three positions in the Residence. Nowhere else did we have such flux and turnover.

Islands

During my first fourteen months in Port-of-Spain, I had an empire of dual accreditations to eight other sparkling and delightful island states: Barbados, St. Vincent, Grenada, Dominica, St. Lucia, St. Kitts, Montserrat, and Antigua. Most were then in halfway house constitutionally and would not become fully independent of the United Kingdom for a few more years. We were able, however, to have direct bilateral dealings with them, especially on development aid. This gave me eager reason to visit most of them two or three times in the period.

When I left Canada to take up this Caribbean post, it was planned to open a new High Commission in Bridgetown, Barbados, in about two years. This office would handle most of the aid work in the region. The Canadian International Development Agency (CIDA) turned out to be in a hurry, however, and I supported their views although it meant losing my other accreditations to Bridgetown sooner than expected. I opposed with vigour, however, CIDA's apparent wish to establish in Barbados a completely self-sufficient aid section that would make large-scale decisions without direct reference to the other High Commissioners in the Eastern Caribbean whose territories would be involved. Their local knowledge and contacts would in that case be largely wasted in a field of primary Canadian policy. Those opposed to the CIDA idea also pointed out that CIDA management in Ottawa could hardly give to Bridgetown the power to make expensive decisions when spending power within CIDA Ottawa was itself so tightly controlled. The battle eventually went to good sense. The abortive scheme had been based on the considerable spending authority of a largely autonomous British office in Bridgetown. We pointed out that this body dealt primarily with Britain's own colonies.

The first of various trips to Barbados was in August 1972 to present my credentials. I handed over a photostat. The original had been sent airmail instead of by courier bag and had got lost in the mails. Mr. Barrow, the Prime Minister, did not seem to notice it was a photostat. Should I confess? Honesty prevailed, and prudence. Somebody would notice later. I explained that the new original was en route by bag. I did not mention that he — and I — were damned lucky even to have a photostat. When the mail loss had been discovered there was just time to give the photo to a new first secretary flying down to our office. He rushed over to my plane at the Trinidad airport and pushed the envelope into my hand just as I was boarding mine to Bridgetown. Close cut. But Barrow probably would not have cared if I had given him a blank piece of paper signed by myself. He was robust, blunt, and unfinicky. He was very interested in Canada and had many ties there. He was anxious to have the new office installed as soon as possible to push and cultivate bilateral interests. As a result of his eagerness combined with CIDA's the new Canadian office in Bridgetown opened in late September 1973. I was caught *à contre-coeur*. I could see the desirability of opening the new post as soon as feasible and worked hard to get this done, including moving our administrative officer from Port-of-Spain to Barbados in early 1973. At the same time I had fallen in love with the charming islands I was about to lose. Indeed the stuff of corny drama — Loved Islands Lost.

One other visit I made to Barbados was to accompany the charming and acute CIDA President, Paul Gérin-Lajoie, for discussions with Barrow and his ministers and to have a look at projects including an imaginative machine to turn sugar cane into cattle feed. I hosted a lunch at a local hotel arranged by our officer from Trinidad. It was a lovely breezy site on the roof of the hotel with splendid sea views. Unfortunately, the breeze was approaching gale scale that day and thus stole some of our aid-related words away including eloquent speeches and toasts. Some of these fine sentiments must have ended up in St. Lucia. Discussions in the corridor are valuable but not if the corridor is a wind tunnel.

Attendance at the Barbados National Day reception in the summer of '73 gave Nina and me an unforeseen pleasure. John and Olive Diefenbaker were prominent guests accompanied by their Barbadian host. But the latter had some other guests to look after so Nina and I lent a hand in shepherd style. We took our adopted guests proudly around and had no problem in lining up eager interlocutors. Dief was in full raconteur form and zestful from having vanquished a sharp bout of illness during a fairly recent visit to Wales. He had a lot of new Welsh blood in him which he found amusing. Proud he should have been, indeed to goodness! He was working on his memoirs in the pastoral surrounds of Barbados. Taking him around was like the big brother lining up dance partners for his kid sister at the school prom. Olive had trouble getting him to go home.

We held our only July 1 reception in Barbados a day or two late, if that does not sound too Irish. On the day itself we had been hosting in Trinidad. In Bridgetown we had an alfresco party in the shell of our future High Commission spread over two floors of an office building. The need to duck around scaffolding and packing cases lent zing to the occasion which was peopled by Bajan VIPs led by the Barrows and the Governor-General as well as a quite large number of charming young Canadian University Service Overseas (CUSO) volunteers in nursing and education. The Barbados lot were pleased to see the brick-and-plaster outward and visible signs of a newborn relationship. Some were kind enough to regret our coming confinement to Trini and expressed surprise that we were not going to switch to Bridgetown. This was Bajan pride at work, an effortless assumption of superiority which extended to our future office. Nina and I explained that we could not move our kids around too often!

When the new separate High Commission in Barbados was imminent in September 1973, I began my farewell calls on my islands of accreditation. The most picturesque were to Grenada and St. Vincent in our chief aid officer's thirty-eight-foot sailboat.

In Grenada I was so awed by the stately lady Governor, who had been absent on leave before, that I asked permission to withdraw as if she were royalty and I practically backed out of the room. An officer accompanying me produced a sparkling limerick on the subject. We saw more of the Prime Minister, Eric Gairy. Nina and I had him to lunch on his own which produced some startling tales of his rise to power from being an oil worker in a Dutch Caribbean island. Gairy entertained us at a reception, then cocktails and dinner, a bit wearing. Feeling rather corrugated the next morning, I just had enough strength left to make history. I became the first envoy ever to swim away from his responsibilities (i.e., to our boat anchored twenty yards offshore from the hotel). So off we sailed up the Grenadine Islands to St. Vincent, making up indecent limericks to spice the lovely tedium of inching past gorgeous but dry little islands.

Despite their name all but the biggest of the Grenadines belong to St. Vincent. For various reasons, we had been there more often than the others. One reason was the articulate bronze Premier, "Son" Mitchell. He ruled by freak. He was the only independent member of the legislature which was otherwise divided by the 1971 election exactly between the two political parties led by Ebenezer Joshua and Milton Cato (a conflict, one might say, between the Old Testament and the Roman Empire). Mitchell became Premier with the support of Joshua's party, a fragile situation that lasted three years. After a Cato government, Mitchell returned to power with a majority of his own. He had a Canadian wife and a University of British Columbia agriculture degree.

For our Easter holidays in 1973 the Reeces had borrowed a cottage on Bequia, a biggish small island next to St. Vincent. It was a cradle of sailors including Mitchell's father. By chance, Mitchell travelled with us on a sailing schooner with motor which was the temporary ferry between the two islands. Mitchell's wife managed a delightful small hotel they owned on Bequia which was fragrantly called the Frangipani. The ferry trip gave me a good chance to discuss affairs of moment with the Premier. He was then head of the association grouping the Eastern Caribbean states. Afterwards I regrettably let some squeam overcome my first instinct to seize this unique chance and send a telegram to Ottawa redolent of the past romance of diplomacy. It would have begun, "As Premier Mitchell and I clung to the rigging of the inter-island schooner, he told me in strict confidence ...." I sent the telegram minus this preface.

Mitchell was the innocent instrument of a religious downfall for the Reece family during our Bequia holiday. He invited us to join him at church and drinks, in that order, on Easter Sunday. The church was stuffed but we were in pews of honour beside the Premier. In the middle of a long prayer with all on their knees, Caroline, then six years old, piped up loud and terribly clear, "What are they all doing, Daddy?" She'd never been at a church service before. Our shame was then finger-pointed. Instead of

In personal sailboat of the senior aid official of the Canadian High Commission in Port-of-Spain.

sifting out in the crowd, we were asked by the vicar in a loud voice from the pulpit to leave first with the Premier — who did not seem too upset about consorting with this ungodly family. But everyone in the congregation watched and knew who this family was who never went to church.

A final snapshot of this Bequia holiday. The Interior and Tourism Minister swooshed up to our beach to give us an invitation straddling his two portfolios. Would we like to come down with him and three female tourism officers in the police launch to stay on Palm Island in the south Grenadines? We would and did. Caroline was discreetly sick in her mother's sun hat during the hot and choppy trip. During a side jaunt later that day we had a child's dream of adventure. We were between two hotelled islands in the launch when it caught fire. Nine-year-old Michael suddenly popped up out of the top hatch of the wheelhouse followed closely by thick black smoke. He had been watching the helmsmanship and was swiftly pushed up and out of danger by a helpful police sailor. The starboard engine was already laid up and useless while the port engine was on fire for reasons unknown. We were drifting near a dangerous reef. One or two of the female passengers skirted hysteria — but not the Reece women! Our children were enchanted by the smoke, drama, and distress rockets. The fire was doused; a rescue boat came out from Palm Island to tow us in safely. Shaken and/or delighted by our day, we fell upon a lobster and rum feast organized by our genially resourceful aid chief. His boat and sundry merry private passengers from Trini on a holiday trip had turned up by coincidence that evening. Because of the police boat wipe-out we had to fly back to St. Vincent the next day in a small bumping plane which accorded ill (the appropriate word), with my liverish state. Nina's hat almost had another customer. Too much lobster in my rum.

On another occasion I damaged our family's reputation for musical appreciation. It was an aid ceremony headlined by myself and Mr. Joshua as Acting Premier at the time. After his gracious speech of welcome and appreciation salted with folk saltiness, which warmly thanked Canada and CIDA for a completed water project, I took the podium with a boring little text from the office. Shedding it, I played for time and inspiration by horrifying my wife. I modestly stated that, unlike myself, she had a fine ear for music and was herself a practitioner. I said that she had just pointed out to me the sparkling quality and calibre of the band playing at the ceremony. This was minor league mischief because even my tin ear had not failed to grasp the low calibre of this highly local band. Fortunately my teasing went unobserved and the band played on. They missed, however, the felicity of playing Handel's *Water Music* while Joshua and I turned the project taps for an arm-twisting length of time.

Dominica

This island was a favourite. After a swoop over green hills the plane turns back and heading seaward again lands on a modest strip. A curvaceous drive past fantastical adolescent mountains brought us to the attractive small capital of Roseau nestled on the sea. The hotel is a converted fort above the sea. Somehow not a very warlike structure.

My presentation of credentials was highly informal since we had left the letter from the Minister back in the hotel. My accompanying officer went chasing back for it while I had a pleasant chat on bilateral relations with an amused Premier Leblanc. The eventual presentation barely interrupted our dialogue. Soon after, I saw in action the doughty Leader of the

Opposition and future Prime Minister, Miss Eugenia Charles, who was castigating the government in the cosy legislature.

Another visit was to attend the fifth anniversary of quasi-independence, Associate Statehood. A state ball was given by the gracious governor, Sir Louis Cools Lartigue. Speeches were made. Mine was not the end of my labours. The guest of chief honour was the Prefect of the neighbouring French island of Guadeloupe. His secretary asked me to translate his speech sentence by sentence. Blessing those who sent me to Quebec, I complied with a touch of class, I thought. But it seemed hardly necessary. The audience reacted to the original not my translation. A French-based patois was common in Dominica.

The end of this Caribbean posting was a tale of three telegrams. I sent them to our personnel dragons in Ottawa from Trinidad's sister, the Island of Tobago, during a long birdwatching weekend with the family in a hotel full of twittering British ornithologists. Our Port-of-Spain office phoned to us a totally unexpected telegram posting us to Ghana. Our initial reaction was that it was time to go home after seven years abroad. So I sent a bleak and categorical "NO" telegram to Ottawa. Then we paced up and down the hills and beaches, re-conning the cons and pros. We would be dually accredited to two French-speaking countries where our Quebec year would score. This might be our only chance to serve in Africa. Katherine could stay in boarding school while the younger children could tolerate a move during primary years as long as the school in Accra was any good. It seemed clear that being High Commissioner in tough places might turn out to be a challenging aspect of an External career as long as we could stand it. The prospect of Ottawa never thrilled any of us; etc., etc.

To the amusement of the communicator in Port-of-Spain, we phoned over to him a sequel telegram for Ottawa the next day. Telegram two was a conditional acceptance of Ghana asking for a guarantee of adequate schooling for the younger kids and two months' leave and training in Canada between tropical posts. As we paced the slopes and beaches some more, however, we grew increasingly attached to the idea of a posting in Ghana and began to fret that the various conditions we had made might snatch the post away. So the less amused communicator was called in for the third time of the long weekend to send a third telegram to Ottawa which said in effect, "Let's Go!" I got a dry reply saying that the Under-Secretary had read my three telegrams and was glad we had accepted. So were we...especially since our conditions had been met.

Our farewell-to-Trinidad dinner was hosted for the government by the Governor-General. He was a new appointment and was a man of charm and wit. Sir Ellis Clarke made a point of entertaining and paying attention to the small corps of ambassadors and high commissioners, deliberately I suspect, to make up for the neglect and coolness of the Prime Minister who was also handling the External Affairs portfolio. Clarke's humour, erudition, and after-dinner eloquence almost caused a small riot at our farewell. After the speeches of some length — I shortened mine — coffee and port were served at the table while the ladies stayed put. This was contrary to the lingering Victorian custom of the country. After the ladies finally withdrew, the host chuckled while the men hustled to an overdue target. After this rather physical moment the evening ended in sweet and jumping music. We literally danced our way off the national stage.

Mrs. Gandhi's Visit To Canada
In 1973 I was called to Ottawa from Trinidad for more than two months to head a task force for the visit to Canada of the Prime Minister of India, Mrs. Indira Gandhi. The early summer visit was to last eight days, three days in Ottawa followed by Toronto, Montreal, the Niagara Region, Banff, Vancouver, and Victoria. My job was to lead a small task force which would prepare and organize the details of the visit and also to steer it. I was told on arrival in Ottawa that some recent high-level visits had not gone well. Regrettably, there had been no one whose head was on the block for the axe if the visit flopped. This one would be different. My head was visible and vulnerable. Welcome back to Ottawa!

When I had left India in 1969, Mrs. Gandhi's position as Prime Minister was fibrillating. As new leader, she was being challenged by the right wing of the Congress party under the ancient ascetic, Morarji Desai. Choice of the next President of India was the major conflict point. Each Congress wing had its own candidate to replace the old Muslim President who had died suddenly. I thought Mrs. Gandhi would lose and become captive or victim of the old experienced Congress *wallahs* who knew every back street tactic. I was entirely wrong. She won with flair. And she won the subsequent national elections with ease. The Nehru loyalties held and the mantle was revitalized by charm lined with tough wiles.

The Ottawa visit went well except for a comic tiff with my conscientious number two in the task force, who had included in the program a reference to Mrs. Gandhi visiting room number sixteen of the House of Commons between engagements there in order to "freshen up." I pulled the text back from the printer to delete these words. Surely they implied she was not already fresh. She got to room sixteen without this guidance.

Security was the major problem throughout the visit. In Ottawa shrill American youngsters hysterically protested a murder charge against their sect's guru in India. They were allowed on one occasion to come too close for comfort — including mine as I was in Mrs. Gandhi's wake. I had strong words to say to the Ottawa Police via the RCMP who had overall responsibility and did a difficult job successfully against a variety of risk makers.

In the Royal York Hotel in Toronto a lunch of one thousand burghers was almost wrecked by a major breach in our security. The organizers asked me before the lunch whether our security chief should sit at the head table. I first thought this would be appropriate and pleasant for him but finally decided against it on the grounds of flexibility. While talking to the mayor's wife at the lunch, well away from the centre of the head table, I heard a strangled but loud squawk from that area. I looked up to see our security chief, an RCMP superintendent of mature years, falling to the floor with a young man he had just tackled while putting a gagging hand to his mouth. The would-be assailant had been in the process of crying out, "Mrs. Gandhi, you are a butcher," so we deduced. He got as far as "butch ...." He was a few feet from his target. He had no gun but a rolled up placard with him. Presumably he had intended to harass or hit her with it. He had walked through the kitchen, which was full of Mounties, unmolested because he was in a white coat and looked like a waiter. I mentally mopped my brow. If our security czar had sat at the head table on its dais, he could not possibly have acted as the last line of defence which held. As it was, the incident was hardly noted in the press — unlike the scragging of Prime Minister Kosygin in Ottawa a year or two earlier.

When the young "waiter" was led away, Mrs. Gandhi cried out, "Don't hurt him." I am told nobody did except her own bodyguard who had to be dragged away from hitting the miscreant in the kitchen. He belonged to the Canadian chapter of an extreme left wing organization popularly known as the "Maoists." They had affinity with Peking, which was then on the outer left of its political curve and enjoying bitter relations with Delhi. The abortive assault had good fruit. When we drove up to the Niagara Shaw Theatre that evening, we saw two men being hustled off, one from each side of the limousine containing the Indian and Canadian Prime Ministers. The RCMP had acted effectively after the Toronto scare and assigned some of their Mao experts to the security detail. They were expert not in the works of Mao but in Canada's Maoists. Thus they had recognized the would-be scraggers in Niagara and effaced them discreetly. This lent piquancy to Trudeau's subsequent joke on stage after the play about its title, *You Never Can Tell*. He referred to the contrasting fortunes of the two Prime Ministers in the preceding two years. His large majority had disappeared into a minority government while her internal party woes had been resolved in a majority win. But Trudeau's jest could also have applied to the security situation.

The security issue continued to dog or scratch at us. In Montreal the RCMP posted policemen at the door of the Ritz Lunch Salon checking out every waiter carrying fodder to Premier Bourassa's elegant lunch for Mrs. Gandhi. The Montreal police lived up to repute by keeping a threatening noisy crowd of demonstrators a full block away from our cars. In Vancouver there was strong concern about potential violence between rival Sikh factions. In the event nothing happened but I had anxious minutes which, in the light of the subsequent assassination of Mrs. Gandhi in Delhi, do not seem too paranoiac. Outside the new Sikh temple a burly young Sikh was sitting in a wheelchair. His right hand was wrapped in a bulky towel. He did not look sick. I pointed him out to the senior security official with the Indian party who checked with the local Sikh leaders. They assured us that the man was both sick and respectable. But I continued to watch him until he finally unwrapped the towel and mopped his brow with it. Later that day I was told that an informer had warned the Mounties that a diversion would be created in one corner of the Vancouver hotel lobby to distract the RCMP while genuine assailants did their work. Needless to say, there was a crop of close-cropped heads in the lobby as Mrs. Gandhi walked through unmolested.

Although security was a *sine qua non*, the importance of the visit lay in the substance. Official discussion in Ottawa went well and Mrs. Gandhi made very effective speeches in Parliament in Ottawa and elsewhere, ending with an address to a British Columbia government dinner in Victoria where fatigue had softened her and she looked like a vulnerable young woman, charming in an orange sari. But mainly she was the iron woman of India. In Banff we provided a few free hours before the final two days of a crammed program in British Columbia. For this leisure period she had a choice of five different tourist and recreation activities. She did all five.

When I said goodbye to Mrs. Gandhi at Trenton Air Base where an Air India jet picked her up, I apologized for the heavy program and thanked her for her forbearance and consideration and courtesy in the face of it. "That's all right, Mr. Reece, it was just like an average week in India." I am sure it was. I sped back to Trinidad with my head intact.

CHAPTER TWELVE

Ghana and West Africa
(1974-76)

IT CAN HONESTLY be said that the Reece family got a charge out of Ghana: we were actually struck by lightning in the state guest house at a hill station three thousand feet above sea-level Accra. At the height of a fierce storm, electrical charges crackled down the lightning conductor of our bungalow as we attempted to maintain a conversation with some guests. Our aplomb evaporated when there was a giant flash and crack. We followed the noise to its focus and found that the lightning had neatly split the loftiest toilet in Ghana. Luckily no one had been enthroned to receive a unique form of hotfoot. The flash had gone right through a plaster wall and part of the earthen floor. After this mighty warning from African Olympus we gave the house servants forty ounces of Beefeater gin before they started the cleanup. We thus had a striking introduction to the West African custom of libation where the ancestors are honoured by the pouring of liquor onto the ground. Few ceremonies we attended took place without this rite.

My official life as High Commissioner in Ghana began with a slightly less whimsical encounter. Soon after arrival I presented my credentials to the Head of State, Colonel Acheampong, and we were then perched on adjacent armchairs for a brief chat. He asked politely about my last post, and, when I told him Trinidad and Tobago, there was a slight pause and a

Katherine and David in a tented safari camp, Kenya, 1975.

Caroline and David in Kenya game park, 1975.

quiet smile on his face. He knew that I knew that he had once served on a tribunal of Commonwealth officers who tried the ringleaders of an abortive military coup in Trinidad. A few years later, in 1972, he had conducted his own coup in Ghana. He had learned how not to do it.

Subsequently, I had a more constructive, if protracted, connection with the Ghanaian military through our involvement in the launching of a much needed senior staff college. While a Ghanaian would of course be first commandant, Canada was originally asked to provide and pay for the seven-man directing staff. This was well beyond our military training funds. Although Canadian help was preferred to British, with its colonial stigma, Ghana eventually arranged to pay for four British officers, whose salaries and allowances were lower than ours, but they could not pay a nickel more in foreign exchange to anyone for the three remaining essential instructors.

After lengthy exploration between Ottawa and Accra on this problem I was so fed up with the situation that I was more than ready for our departure *en famille* for a planned Kenya safari. Luckily, Ethiopian Airlines lost an engine en route to Accra and our trip was delayed by two days. So I recogitated the staff college question and came up with the obvious solution. I persuaded the Ghanaians to pay the purely local costs for our colonels in local currency. As a result, the foreign exchange costs proved to be just within our military assistance budget. The college was saved.

Was it worth it? I think so. The country needed mature and well-trained officers of senior rank in the immediate circumstances of a military government. In terms of human rights, the benefits from substantial contact with high-calibre Canadian officers would be valuable. It might be asked in general why Canada had a substantial development aid program in a country whose government was sometimes inept and corrupt. The answer? The ordinary Ghanaian needed our aid and the government, while not exactly benign to its opponents, held together a country of diverse tribes subject to centrifugal forces in the aftermath of the breakdown of the Nkrumah years. Acheampong was a modest and uncharismatic leader. His one crowd ploy was a waved handkerchief. With gallantry he waved it when he was led to the firing squad after the coup against the régime.

A controversial aid problem arose in my last year in Ghana. A number

of senior and influential aid officials in Ottawa were opposed to con-
tributing to an extension of the Volta dam project unless the U.S. aluminum smelter companies paid more for their power. The biggest users,
these companies had long-term, low-cost contracts with the Ghanaian government. It seemed improper to contemplate a second dam even though
more electrical capacity was badly needed in the country. The U.S. companies finally agreed to an increase in power prices despite their contracts
and the proponents of the Kpong dam won the day. My own urging that
Ottawa participate was slightly influenced by the powerful arguments of
the formidable chief of the Ghana hydro authority who was a neighbour
and friend. (Despite my considerable skill at the game, his ten-year-old son
thrashed me regularly at ping-pong. A tough family.) I was spurred over
Kpong by the fact that Canadian participation seemed to be regarded by
the World Bank as a condition for their own investment which was essential to the whole project. The dam was built.

The Volta dam project was the scene of a gross pun I laid on our then
Foreign Minister, Allan MacEachen, during his official visit to Ghana in
1975. As we walked through the powerhouse at the dam I suggested that
he must feel right at home there. He was perplexed. "Why?" ... "The corridors of power." He grunted amiably. He was less amused when for two
days running, his motorcycle escorts fell off their steeds at speed and damaged themselves. For the rest of his program he was spared African hexes.
He had useful talks, a state dinner, and a working supper with Ghanaian
ministers at our residence, as well as a reception in the garden for as many
Canadians as we could find.

One visiting Canadian journalist came through Accra at short notice just
before we were setting off on an official trip. I was able to see her only
briefly in the office but her subsequent newspaper article made me glad we
had not entertained her lavishly. On the other hand a fuller briefing might
have helped. In her exaggerated article she described the moderate military government of Ghana as wielding the "guns of dictatorship" and
added some equally overblown criticism of its family planning efforts.
There was mention of natives with human teeth necklaces and other such
choice hints at barbarism. These accounts unfortunately ended with high
praise for the Canadian High Commissioner. It all looked as if I had

Canadian Residence tennis court and hut, Accra.

stimulated her comments or that she had been parroting the views of the excellent envoy! I hoped the Ghanaian High Commissioner in Ottawa had the good sense not to send the article to home base. An old Ghana hand living in Toronto wrote a neat put-down letter to the newspaper and that was it.

In point of fact, the guns of dictatorship were very visible once a year at the highest level but they were not loaded. At a special ceremony the Head of State led his cabinet ministers, all serving officers, in an intricate parade ground military drill exercise. In vivid scarlet uniforms, with a snappy band, their smart and meticulous display reminded the public that these men were still soldiers with the armed forces behind them.

But they did not stay that way. The military régime lost the support of its own rank and file a few years after we left Ghana. The men we had seen drilling on the parade ground were executed on the same site. Perhaps their emphasis on the military while in office was a fatal mistake. It made them seem accountable to their junior colleagues. More emphasis on the civilian burden they carried *pro bono publico* might have been less provocative to the sergeants, corporals, and privates who unseated them.

Ghana was a good place for outdoor diplomatic activity. One locale was the Residence tennis court and its adjoining refreshment shelter, the little grass hut as we called it. It was too hot to play before 5:00 P.M. but this was just the right time for my partner and me to have one set with the sun in our opponents' eyes before it set behind the bulky Residence and we could change ends and turn on the lights. Such *droit de seigneur* tactics were needed for my slightly better than feeble game. Selection of strong partners was another must. The real game of tennis diplomacy was played after the last set as we soaked up a gin or two in the little grass hut under the lights. It was a full tropical night by 6:00 P.M. all year round in a land so near the equator. Our suburban neighbourhood was feebly lit. Once I asked a regular partner, Ernest Ako, who was the Interior Minister and Inspector General of Police, if he worried about sitting under our spotlight. "Ernest, you missed a game here a few weeks ago because you had been busy scotching a coup attempt which was to feature you as chief hostage. What kind of security is this?" He replied quietly, "I'm not as alone as you think, David." Visions of eyes and guns staring at us from the ambient dark of the African night.

I received crucial aid from my tennis friend Ako in an amusing but important defence of Ghanaian and Canadian interests. Canadian aid was building a technical college at Kumasi, capital of the central region and second city of Ghana. The project was being held up because the city was dumping night soil on college land earmarked for the final and essential stage of construction. The Mayor of Kumasi was a bustling army major who had more influence than his rank. He refused to stop the daily load until the central government provided a new and adequate site for the unstoppable output of its own citizens.

I began my campaign locally. I briefed the Regional Commissioner (i.e., executive governor) who had not been told the facts before. More importantly, I briefed the King of the Ashantis (i.e., their paramount chief, the Asantahene) who had been their temporal ruler until the British came and overcame fierce resistance. He still had important influence and was recognized formally as the leader of the paramount chiefs. A lawyer and former cabinet minister, he was distressed to learn of the stopped-up situation. Returning to Accra, I spoke to the Minister of Education who was, like Ako, a police officer. His heart was in the right place but I was not sure he had the fire power. So I spoke to Ako. The impasse was uncorked. The combination of local potentate, who knew well the importance of the project to the region, and the authority of a very senior minister who belonged to the same service as the minister responsible, was enough to stop the flow. During my next visit to Kumasi I received a dirty look from the mayor but I believe his concerns were soon met elsewhere. Nina said I should be made Knight of the Soil. In fact the Ghana government did offer me a decoration subsequently. As usual, our own government did not allow me to accept a foreign decoration.

Apart from earthy puns and heroic work on the school board of the International School, Nina learned much and had fun as a student at the Institute of African Studies at Legon University, just outside Accra. Her music course included instruction on the African xylophone. We had an authentic one sent down from northern Ghana and, after many years, donated it to Carleton University. We had a surprising number of visitors and a heavy load of entertaining in a house which looked like a battle cruiser made of brick and stucco. Dinners and lunches were prepared by our French African cook from Togo. All this activity took the usual careful arranging and supervision, with my only contribution ... the table plan. Supplies were very short and great ingenuity was required to keep food on the table for guests, family, and servants.

Our two youngest children loved Ghana in spite of their rather feeble school. Son Michael made a soccer pitch out of our ample garden where barefoot African kids divided up and played with shrill élan. Michael was also unshod, pointing out that his ball control was better that way. Snakes again ... but no damage resulted. He was not so lucky in our Egyptian embassy neighbour's garden when he fell on a freshly pruned rose branch and punctured his cheek. Since I was busy in a high-level tennis match with some cabinet ministers on the home court, I got Nina out of a school board meeting. Wounds are woman's work. She hustled him to the nearby military hospital and he was expertly stitched up. I got a lecture on work equity. But my chief critic was our courtly Muslim gardener who underwent much suffering and travail at first from the soccer games. He was horrified by the presence of the local riffraff of boys. I had to use my best-honed negotiating skills to keep him happy, and we put the grass to rights before our departure.

Michael and Caroline also played Little League baseball and the piano. They made and fielded hits in both spheres. After getting rapped on the knuckles, Caroline dismissed her piano teacher (with Nina's permission). Michael played a duet with our neighbour's ping-pong genius at a concert. After this untalented performance, the teacher gently suggested they turn their energies elsewhere. Michael hit out in self-defence during a jeep ride in a rather sparse game park in West Ghana. By his count he killed forty-five tsetse flies. Their bite can cause encephalitis. We did not get it. Home run for Michael.

Compared to most others we have known, the Accra Residence had very moderate security. No grills, no electronic screamers on the doors, no push-button alarms, no safe havens, and a glass door only at the foot of one staircase. There were two outside guards but they were usually asleep in the hallowed tradition of such characters. The veteran at the front was not amused by my occasional insomniac strolls in the small hours around the garden. One night he told me with rancour that never in eighteen years on the job had he been woken and scolded as I had done. Three hours later our family was aroused by our tropicalized labrador, a sturdy dog called Christo. His persistent barking alerted us to mischief below. I called out to Ali the guard who responded by fetching a ferocious bow and arrow which he pointed at the front door. Our maid then called out that the "chop room" (dining room) doors were open. I invited Ali to take his archery over there. For once his adequate grip on English failed him. He shook his head and stayed put. Finally we went down to the dining room and found the French door forced, an easy job. A couple of minor items had been stolen. More would have been gone but for Christo. Stimulated by his bark and perhaps his bite, the thief had fled so swiftly that he had left his running shoes behind. A policeman investigating the crime noted that the inner door knob of the escape route was all "blawd" — not Christo's work, however. The policeman meant "blurred" fingerprints not "blood." We had forgotten our Agatha Christie and touched the evidence. The thief was never found but Ali was a little less surly about being woken up thereafter.

During our stay in Ghana we grew close to a paramount chief and his family. He was high in the tribal hierarchy. Although not temporal rulers,

David at a ceremony at the palace of the Ochenehene, Paramount Chief, near Accra, 1976.

the paramount chiefs exerted considerable influence among their tribes and the government consulted them through their organization of chiefs presided over by the Asantehene. The next in importance was the Ochenehene. His family, the Ofori-Attas, had been distinguished in previous civilian governments. One had been my Ghanaian opposite number in New Delhi and we had lumbered around the tennis court together in the murderous summer heat. It makes a bond. We discovered another one. Alex Ofori-Atta suffered badly from gout. I kept my gout away with a pill a day. On my advice it worked for him too.

When he discovered us in Ghana he invited us to three consecutive ceremonies at his chief's palace, a large but rather decrepit dwelling. The first ceremony celebrated final funeral rites for the previous chief. Other diplomats were there. Two of them slipped quietly away before the last act of salutation and the greeting to the new ruler. They had omitted to bring with them the *de rigueur* gift of libation material for the chief. I barely survived this important ritual because I had packaged my six assorted bottles myself in haste before leaving Accra. As I advanced across the ceremonial grounds the vari-shaped vessels began to slide in opposite directions in their rag-tag wrappings. I had to carry this awful bundle up fifty steps in the near dark to where the next Ochenehene sat enthroned. By desperate juggling I just averted a mass libation and soaking tribute to the gods and the chief on the staircase.

At the second Ochenehene ceremony my family and I were the only foreign guests. I had a chat afterwards with the chief who seemed a very pleasant, youngish man who had spent some time in the U.K. as a school teacher. His companion, an Ofori-Atta, was also robed in Kente cloth of vivid silk. He was a former finance minister. A month later my friend Alex phoned me in grief from the Accra hospital. The paramount chief had died suddenly and unexpectedly of an internal affliction. I did not enjoy the third tribal ceremony where again we were the sole foreigners. We walked past the bier where the dead chief lay with a piece of wood between his teeth. We never met the new chief. The lengthy and intricate process of selection from eligible near relatives was still going on when we left Accra, a process in which the queen mother plays a big part.

At the second ceremony before the chief's death we had been accompanied by the mother of our friend Chris Young. She was our house guest but did not need any briefing from us about Ghana. Fifty years earlier Grace Young and her husband, Norman, had spent three or four years in Ghana teaching at a new boys' school with an international faculty. (Norman later founded Ravenscourt in Winnipeg.) The Youngs had stayed in a mission school in the hill station we used, learning Ewe in order to help with boarders from that area. When she visited the former mission, now a government teachers' college, she was astonished to find on the same wall of the same room they had occupied fifty years before the same framed picture of the Rockies they had left there as a gift.

The school in Accra where Mr. Young taught, Achimota, shared instructors with an affiliated teachers' college. One of the students at the college was Kwame Nkrumah, spearhead of anti-colonialism in Africa and first president of Ghana. Shortly before full independence Mrs. Young visited Ghana and called on Nkrumah who was then chief minister. He received her with charm. "Of course I remember Mr. Young very well. He gave me two very important gifts. One was a love of history and the other a strong taste for the public stage. He was the first teacher under the colonial régime to research and instruct African history. He also directed a John Drinkwater play about Lincoln. I played Lincoln." Nkrumah's remarks about history were echoed to me by a history professor of Cape Coast University who said his own career as an African historian had been much stimulated by Norman Young's research.

HISTORICAL NOTE: My old school friend Chris Young was the first foreign baby born in colonial Ghana. The colonial mothers all went home for a comfy accouchement but Grace Young was too busy. In the Accra hospital she was told to bite hard on a piece of wood and on no account to cry out in pain. There were sick men in an adjoining ward who must not be disturbed! She obeyed. Chris acquired the Ghanaian birth name Kofi, born on Friday. His family called him nothing else. But when he blossomed as a correspondent, editor, and columnist his by-line became a more prosaic Christopher.

During our posting a more professional thespian than Nkrumah became our neighbour (i.e., her residence was next to our office in Accra). Shirley Temple Black was a successful and charming ambassador whose sojourn in Ghana was almost the same span as ours. We had met in New York through membership in a United Nations environment committee and she had cocktailed in our Park Lane eyrie. This gave Nina and myself the excuse to meet her at the airport on her arrival. This is Not Done. Envoys do not officially exist until they have presented credentials. The U.S. chargé outraged some senior diplomats by sending an official note giving her arrival time, thus implying an invitation to break this rule. The fact that she was a woman, an American, and a former child movie star doubtlessly added to the choler of the stuffier excellencies.

Thus only a brave small band turned up at the airport. The Yugoslav and Egyptian envoys said their heads of state had met and been charmed by her. They were present by presidential wish — although I doubt if they had sought special instructions. I was there as neighbour twice over and former United Nations colleague. Awaiting the Temple flight, my colleagues and I keenly speculated on the position of one envoy whose country had close relations with the U.S. He was a very senior member of our diplomatic corps and thus especially vulnerable to crabbing from the old crusties if he turned up. From the new VIP lounge we perked up as we saw his flag and two passengers in his car approach and stop well away from the entrance to the lounge, down a sloping drive. After a few minutes the car turned and started to drive away again. Clearly prudence and chilly feet had taken over at the sight of crowds and cameras blazing. But the car seemed to hover for a moment as it passed out of our sight below. Diplomacy of enormous subtlety was revealed as we saw the envoy's wife toiling up the slope alone in the hot sun to greet Shirley.

Ambassador Black told us later that we were the only people to give her a welcome dinner in Ghana. The party seemed rather sparkly despite a slipped-disc attack which had kept me in bed for two days before the dinner. My relaxer pills for my back and the whisky taken to counteract them almost put me to sleep on the delightful bosom of the cabinet minister's wife beside me. (I had made Shirley as guest of honour the co-host at the other end of the table — a protocol twist she doubtlessly remembered when she became chief of protocol in Washington two years later.) I managed to shrug off my torpor in time to make a toast after dinner which was said to be apt and not too somnolent.

Shirley was an attractive and intelligent envoy with an understandable flair for publicity. Her husband Charlie Black was bright and humorous, and a solid supporter of Shirley's career. He came through Accra often but was still based in California pursuing far-flung business interests. Quite rightly she never discussed her past and early glories — unless you raised the subject. As a matter of professional pride I never did — but listened closely if someone else did. Thus I know how she learned her lines when she was too young to read. Her mother read them to her at bed-time and at wake-up, and they remained imprinted until the scene was shot. Shirley was away from Accra when a prominent film producer arrived with a small entourage including a rather lugubrious screen writer. They called on me for lack of Shirley. They were planning to make a film about an African state with a very nasty military régime. They were confident they could make it in Ghana. I pointed out that Ghana itself had a military government, although admittedly moderate and quite amiable. There was another twist in the plot about a minority tribal leader which would also make an African locale of any kind hard to find. This soothsaying was on target. The film was finally made on another continent.

Ghana was a country of much interest and variety both in landscape and culture. Thus it was almost always exciting and rewarding to travel outside of Accra, either by car or plane. A little more exciting by plane because of bouncing around in small craft in prickly weather. Sometimes challenging by car since our driver favoured detours to check up on his far-flung progeny. On holidays and weekends when we drove ourselves, our bright red Peugeot wagon would be crammed with enough cargo for a small hotel.

For our Easter holiday weekend we had booked a VIP guest house near Half Assini near the western border of Ghana and Ivory Coast. The area had been Nkrumah's home base. Hence, a splendid guest chalet was there. Through the right bureaucratic channels we had sought our reservation and received confirmation by telegram two weeks in advance. Then an hour before departure, and in the middle of winding down an unavoidable official lunch at the Residence, we received a terse telegram from the local authorities saying our stay would be impossible. The electrical generator was broken and thus our reservations had to be cancelled. But our car was half-packed by the kids who were jumping with expectation. No other holiday site was feasible at such short notice. So we used the Bobby Kennedy technique: when the Cuban missile crisis was at grave danger point he suggested the United States answer a conciliatory Kruschev telegram rather than the subsequent bellicose one. It worked. And for us too. We set off clutching the confirmation telegram.

A day later we arrived at the splendid guest house. It was in fact no longer splendid but very run-down and ill-equipped with a non-working refrigerator. It was, however, just livable and near a charming beach adorned with a rust-eaten old shipwreck. It was said that its captain committed suicide from intense chagrin at making such an elementary error of navigation. And the electricity worked fine. Among the local functionaries who called on us was the superintendent of electricity who told us over a drink that he was staying on duty all weekend to ensure effective generation. Perhaps he had sent the second telegram!

On the way back we took a guided tour of the old fort at Elmina which was Portuguese and then British. It was originally used to house slaves awaiting passage across the Atlantic. The guide told us that an adjoining village had a few residents of mixed ancestry. He explained that past governors had slept with comely slaves who were liberated in the village when they became pregnant. An indignant voice rang out: "Not the British governors!" It was a fellow tourist who turned out to be the wife of a prominent British politician.

On official trips our car was crammed with goodies for the Canadians we would meet in the remotest villages. I always considered it essential to my job that I talk to Canadians in the field, missionaries of various caste, volunteers for the many non-governmental agencies, as well as people employed by companies working on CIDA contracts, usually called cooperants. In Ghana, a country of seven languages as well as English, with poor communications, scattered Canadians could be valuable informants. Nina usually came along to set up the parties and to add a sympathetic ear to the very real hardships of these wonderful Canadians.

On business and official tours we visited the northernmost regional capital, Bolgatanga, three or four times. Once when the beer ran out there we crossed the border to Ouagadougu, the capital of Upper Volta (now Burkino Fasso), where the French and African élite had a well-stocked supermarket. Ouagadougu is a city of the traditional contrasts, government buildings attractive in stark modernity, and cone-like African mosques: steel and glass vs. ancient shapes from the local soil. We also took the spur trip across the border to learn more about the United Nations' "river blindness" (an eye disease) program centred in Ouagadougu and including Ghana in its scope.

There were many Canadians in northern Ghana. Some were engineers and their families, concerned with an extensive and excellent CIDA water project in the region. Many hundreds of wells were dug by the big rigs and crews in villages, small towns, and other nodal points to provide potable water and to cut the traditional drudgery of women carrying pots of it on their heads for miles. Other Canadians were White Fathers, an active group from Quebec who had been missionaries and teachers in the area for many years. They had long provided the local Catholic bishop. En route to the northwestern sector of Ghana we stopped at one village to meet the remarkable total of eleven Canadians who worked in this utterly remote corner. Most of them were White Fathers, others cooperants. One brother showed us with pride a photo of a church he had helped to build in 1935.

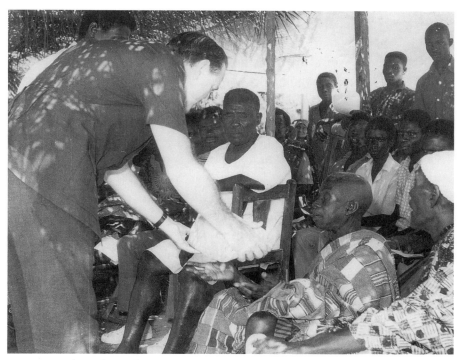

The author making a presentation to a village elder in Ghana in 1974.

Since then he had been back to Canada only once. He was Francophone but his French had gone rusty in the reign of local languages. The White Fathers spanned the border with Upper Volta which was one reason why the bilingual Quebec Fathers were so useful. We met one at the order's headquarters in Ouaga who was performing the fairly rare feat of recovering from virulent blackwater fever. His main concern was that he might not be allowed to continue his mission in Africa.

Motoring west on this trip through the fine red dust, we stayed with a Canadian religious group which also had a school at the town of Wa, the area administrative centre and seat of the important local Muslim chief, the Wa Na of Wa. He was an ancient spry joker. He received us under a regal canopy outside his mud and brick palace which reminded me of Yeats — "of clay and wattles made." The Wa Na pointed out that I was a great man of water (i.e., the wells project). Therefore, I had the power to make it rain.

Please do so immediately. I explained that my powers were rather weak in the morning but gained strength during the day. I could guarantee, therefore, that the rain would fall soon after my departure. The Wa Na seemed to enjoy this banter exchanged in stately fashion through an interpreter. And I was amused to be included among those revered African savants, the rain makers. The ruler invited us to his spring festival but, alas, we did not make it.

The canopy of the Wa Na was not solely for my benefit. In fact I think it was mainly for the benefit of the Ghanaian Minister of Information and Broadcasting who was touring the area with a long train of senior companions from his ministry. He had been the lion at a dinner we had attended the night before given by the northern region commissioner. He was an army officer, whose main base was at Bolgatanga. The lion roared at the inexperienced and bad service of the local staff. They had capped his irritation with a glass of iceless and neat gin instead of the frosty gin and tonic he craved after a hot dusty day. The commissioner's attractive young wife sought whispered advice and sympathy from Nina who at one point of the minister's angry bad manners said loudly, "You don't frighten me, Colonel X." But he clearly frightened everyone else including his companions from Accra. We knew him well and he was an amiable and agile member of our tennis sessions. But we heard some tales of bullied subordinates. He was executed in the subsequent coup because of his top position in the military hierarchy. This made his death inevitable even if he had been the milk of military sweetness.

One of the ways we had of entertaining Canadians in Ghana was to invite all those we knew about to National Day parties in Accra on or about July 1st. (At this time our allowances were adequate to meet such expensive outlays plus the year-round entertainment treadmill.) In 1975 we gave a standard noon reception for officials, and in the evening a film show of the movie Kamouraska based on the novel by Quebec writer Anne Hébert which we knew and admired. The film reached us only the evening before and we had time to see only the first half. Since the book and film were called Kamouraska I mentioned in my few remarks of welcome to my guests that there was a Catholic sister from Kamouraska in the audience. I regretted this remark when the second half of the film displayed more explicit sex than I had remembered from the book read a few years before and certainly not minimized in the movie adaptation. After the film the small group of nuns from central Ghana left rather hastily. A Canadian priest from that region whom we knew well said, "Don't worry, David, they see it all the time in the ditches!"

From my post in Ghana I also had three other accreditations to neighbouring countries, in keeping with a common practice of grouping responsibilities rather than having full diplomatic representation in every country. As in the Caribbean, I would visit the other accreditations regularly as well as on special occasions, dealing with bilateral business, consulting with government and opposition leaders, if any, seeking information from diplomats and journalists living *in situ*, and generally looking after Canadian interests and keeping in touch with Canadian nationals while making use of their views in understanding the countries concerned. From Ghana I covered Liberia, Benin, and Togo, the two latter being former French colonies.

A few months before I left Ghana, the accreditation to Liberia was switched to my office and, before I was able to present my credentials, I was required to represent Canada at the inaugural of President Tolbert. He had formerly been vice-president to the legendary Tubman. There I met another legend, the giant Idi Amin, President of Uganda. He was present as head of the Organization for African Unity. I was hauled out of my hotel swimming pool to make it more secure for Amin. At the opening church service for the inaugural celebrations, where Tolbert and Amin sat facing the congregation of foreign envoys, a leading African churchman gave a trenchant sermon which lambasted colonialism and imperialism, etc., hardly a surprise. But then he switched to evils in modern Africa — tyranny, cruelty, dictatorship, corruption, brutality, etc. Amin looked unhappy while a tiny smile flickered on the edge of President Tolbert's lips. This turned off when the clergyman, a Liberian, said more progress had been made in ten years of independence in some African countries than in 140 years of Liberian nationhood.

When I did get to present credentials in Liberia, the chief of protocol kept me waiting for an hour at my hotel. I was in more of a sweat than normal, worried that I was keeping President Tolbert waiting. I was not. I waited another forty minutes after reaching the palace with the ineffable chief of protocol. This was African time. Finally, after a relaxed little ceremony in a very large room, Tolbert asked me to join him in a trip to a rubber estate where we lunched with its American managers. The president seemed a pleasant man, personally sensitive and considerate, progress or no progress. So was his Foreign Minister, Dennis, who detected that I was not feeling well and offered to arrange a medical appointment. I was very sorry that both leaders died in the coup a year or two later. Tolbert was killed in the attack on his palace. Dennis was among those executed by overzealous soldiers on the beach at Monrovia. Future events were to prove tragic for Liberia.

At the Dahomey National Day celebrations in 1974, I witnessed the official transformation of the once French colony of Dahomey into the Marxist-Leninist state of Benin. The celebrations featured a lurid pageant from the past depicting whites whipping slaves and other graphic sketches of the colonial period. When I called soon afterwards on the Minister of National Guidance, a young Gendarmerie officer, he asked me what I had thought of the pageant which had upset some other Western envoys. I replied that my recent posting in the Caribbean had brought home to me the cruel past and the deplorable legacy of slavery including the problem of people lost and uprooted, and the economic handicap of one-crop economies left by the plantation past. The Caribbean people were looking to their African heritage and seeking identity and roots here. But their African cousins were not responding. The only African leader who had shown any interest asked me how to get Canadian banks to operate in Ghana as they did in the West Indies. I asked the young Benin minister why there were so few ties between the African cousins. He seemed impressed by my points but did not answer my question. He was said to be a dedicated Marxist but the other ministers I dealt with seemed to be the same old moderate army officers they were before the national change of political stripe. They were also very polite. When my slightly stumbling French once stumbled a bit too much, the minister said that French was also not their first language. But it often sounded so.

France retained much influence in Benin despite its lack of Marxist-Leninist sympathies. Their able and simpatico ambassador had much to do

Reece with Togo and Benin cabinet ministers at lunch in Lomé after ceremony to open Ghana, Benin and Togo electricity project with Canadian CIDA support, 1976.

with this success. He was always helpful and available to me, and highly well-informed. Although he may have suffered from Reece French, he only switched once to his excellent English (learned with the British forces in World War II) and that was when we were discussing a sensitive topic in a crowded restaurant.

The American ambassador was also hospitable. He was not steeped in Africa but he was an expert on Marxism. I think he found the Benin leaders rather lacking in knowledge of their chosen political system. A pity he could not have given them lessons!

Togo is a slice of country about thirty miles wide at the coast. I sometimes had breakfast in Accra, an official lunch in Lomé, capital of Togo, and dinner in Cotonou with a Canadian cooperant or a resident ambassador. The whole trip, minus the meals, was about five and a half hours at a medium pace. I grew so used to this voyage that I swore that the same topless crone was always standing at the same fork of the same road every time we passed by. The only thing we hit was a goat, quite gently, during this frequent crisscrossing.

Unlike Liberia, which had too much per capita income to qualify for Canadian aid, Benin and Togo were part of our CIDA program in Francophone Africa. We had, for example, built a sturdy technical college in Benin. On behalf of the cooperants assigned to projects in these countries as well as other Canadians, we decided to have back-to-back National Day parties in Cotonou and Lomé, following our celebrated film show in Accra. With our kids, who too often got left behind, we headed for a short family visit to a hotel in Cotonou, trailing an office van of party fare across the borders. The Third Secretary from Accra came under his own steam. In a cooperant's rented house, the party in Benin was well attended and fun but marked by the attempt of one guest, too long deprived of good Canadian rye whisky, to drink a whole bottle. He almost made it before gastric retribution overtook him.

When in Lomé to give the second party, we learned that rioting had broken out in Benin just after we left. I sent our driver dashing back to Accra in the official car with a report to Ottawa and carried on in the van. I got the inside story of the riots through a European diplomat based in Benin who had come to shop in the abundant French-supplied supermarket of Lomé — worth a detour as the guidebooks say. He had briefed our gourmand third secretary among the cheeses, fresh raspberries, and wine.

We hosted the second, bigger party in a Lomé hotel and it started out very sedately. It then moved on to a Canadian's house and burst out in all directions. I remember Africans gathering quietly outside the house to watch with amusement — or scorn — the dancing shenanigans of benighted foreigners. We rattled back to the hotel in the office van as the sun came up over the old Slave Coast.

Later in the day we were left at the mercy of the Togo taxi industry when the van had to go off with another message, the telephone situation not having improved. African taxi drivers are bred in the bone fast and reckless, but the king of them all befell the Reece family that day. From our hotel by the sea a few miles from Lomé, we had all gone into town for drinks with the cheery American ambassador, who saw to it that the children were entertained and fed in her study during our exchange of views.

Talks over, we set off in the night back to the hotel by taxi. The driver soon began careening along the pitch dark road which dropped down to a few feet beside the sea with dangerously unprotected shoulders or descended into jolting potholes. A dim light caught the sight of waves now and then. The journey grew so dangerous that I started yelling at the taxi driver. I finally made a slight impact by pointing out that I was seeing the Foreign Minister and the President the next day (half true) and would denounce the driver's treatment of the Canadian ambassador and family. He slowed his pace marginally, although he clearly did not believe that any ambassador would be so dumb and bereft as to take his taxi. Almost trembling with relief at deliverance at the door of our hotel some nerve-wracking minutes later, I paid the now smiling wretch only to realize shortly afterwards that he had massively short-changed me. Too late. He had already hurtled into the night, having punished me financially for that cock-and-bull ambassador story, an insult to his credulity.

Luckily I had my own car back for a trip to Lomé later in 1975 to promote the candidature of a Canadian running for the office of head of a United Nations agency. Unfortunately, I was not in top shape for this assignment, having been struck down by food poisoning in Accra the day before. I was in feeble form for the official dinner I had to host in Lomé for our candidate. Shriven and shaky, I had some difficulty stumbling through my toast in French. The candidate, who was an old acquaintance, suggested to me afterwards that my teacher in Quebec must have been called Diefenbaker. This stung a little. Awakened early in a frigid hotel room, I polished a few phrases for use in our interview later that morning with President Eyedema, a robustly blunt army man. In French I introduced the candidate "as a leader like you, Mr. President — although in a sphere much more restricted — a man of strength, wisdom, candour, vigour, integrity, etc." This did not get Togo's vote — it turned out they were already committed — but it went down well. We were invited to leave our hard chairs in front of the President's desk and to take relaxed refreshments with him in an adjoining room. "If only we had two votes …" he mused with regret. Afterwards the candidate told me maybe there was something to be said for a year of French in Quebec.

Farewell

We were posted home in 1976. Our last glimpse of Ghana was twelve hours late thanks to a British Caledonia plane leaking cargo. The Reece caravan eventually arrived at the airport to find some faithful friends and colleagues still turning up to say goodbye. Drinks were happily provided by Ghanaian protocol in their very VIP lounge. Shirley Temple Black arrived in a drenching shower but her hairdo was saved by gallant husband Charlie who took his shirt off to cover her head. At this farewell, having exhausted other topics in the wearing ritual of saying goodbye to people you will probably never see again, I pushed little Caroline forward and told Shirley she was thinking of a stage career. Shirley won a small heart and eased the sorrow of leaving — Caroline had just told me Ghana had been her favourite posting — by suggesting to me, "Just let me know when she's ready and I'll fix things up!" Caroline's waning theatrical urge has still left this cheque blank.

The final stage out of Ghana was slapstick. During our posting the Canadian government had cut all first-class travel previously accorded to heads of posts and family on the way to their posts for the first time and on their departure. We had been glad of this perk during a much-delayed and very tedious trip to Ghana in 1974. My family knew of the change of status but the Ghanaian protocol chief automatically drove us in their official stretch Mercedes right to the first-class front of the aircraft. The family headed swiftly to the rear door as the chief of protocol urged them into first class. I finally persuaded him that all was okay and we went our separate ways.

Ghana Postscript

The first glimpse I had of Africa had been the wrong place. In 1966 the delegation and journalists accompanying Prime Minister Pearson to the Commonwealth Conference in Lagos were tucked into a large air force jet. As we landed, the pilot told us we were in Ghana not Nigeria. The headwinds had been too strong to permit the planned non-stop hop. The journalists amused themselves by vocally imagining Pearson saluting the wrong city, country, and leader on arrival. Despite the very brief notice the Ghanaians excelled themselves in an escalating welcome scenario. The chief of state protocol was on deck to greet us at the foot of the ramp. He was a relegated minister whose wife had attracted delighted western publicity by buying a golden bed. Not in Nkrumah's socialist image. The protocol chief made it clear to me that he would rather be in bed this early Sunday morning. His brow was painfully furrowed after a night of strenuous "high life" dancing and refreshment. But he was still efficient and had the plane swiftly moved to a special airport welcome terminus for heads of state and government. The foreign minister was already in place there and ten minutes later President Nkrumah arrived in long white trousers, sidetracked from his early morning tennis. He swept Pearson off for a tour of Accra and a chat. Out of disgust with British policy in Rhodesia — and perhaps a twinge of jealousy about the Nigerian hosts — Nkrumah was boycotting the Lagos conference. But he told Pearson, "If anybody can make sense of it, you can, Mike." Pearson liked Nkrumah but claimed to be immune to such flattery. He added a wry anecdote for us about once being cooped up with his wife in a small bedroom in the British Prime Minister's country house, Chequers, while all the remaining guest quarters were occupied by Nkrumah and his security men.

Our Accra visit included a tour for the lesser lights but this ended on a note of irritation. In error we were kept in the terminus waiting for Pearson but he was already on the plane, champing to get off to Lagos and not keep our hosts there waiting any longer. When we finally got to the plane, we had to file penitently past him one by one since he was in the front row seat. The prince of dirty looks was bestowed on us. The genial Mike could get highly irritated.

CHAPTER THIRTEEN

Ottawa and Vienna
(1976-82)

I FELT LIKE Rip Van Winkle in Ottawa after nine years' absence. As Director of the Caribbean and then the South Asian Divisions, I worked on our relations with areas well-known to me from the field, but the paper shuffling, meetings, and endless phone calls to clear, coordinate, and obtain approval appealed to me even less than before. I did help to put through one concrete and important decision, the restoration of a useful full-scale aid program to India. It had been cut to food and agricultural aid only, after their nuclear explosion of 1974 used material thought to have come from a reactor constructed with Canadian help but not fully safe-guarded. The rest of my work in Ottawa was chicken feed.

My spirits perked up one day when Michael and Caroline solemnly told me that they would be very willing to head out again on a posting. Having just been passed over for a senior job in Ottawa, I was susceptible to this junior league suggestion. A few months later we flew off in June 1978 for a seven-year stretch in Vienna and Jamaica. Vienna was our seventh home in a decade — the seventies shuffle. I was Ambassador and Head of Delegation to the Mutual and Balanced Force Reduction Talks (MBFR). This was a NATO/Warsaw Pact negotiation aimed at a treaty to reduce armed forces on both sides and build confidence through effective verification of reductions and such means as mutual notification and observation of

MBFR ambassadors at an official lunch in Vienna. The host, USA ambassador Jock Dean, is on the left of the front row. David is on the far left of the back row.

manoeuvres. The MBFR had been chugging away for five years already. The protagonist negotiators were ambassadors of NATO and the Warsaw Pact countries with territory in the region of Europe where the force reductions were to take place. They included both Germanies, Belgium, the Netherlands, Luxembourg, Czechoslovakia, and Poland. The other participants were the countries with forces in the reduction area; namely, the United States, the Soviet Union, the United Kingdom, and Canada. The remaining Alliance members, except France which stayed out, rejoiced in the informal and anatomical title of "flank countries." But in the NATO group at least they played a full role in the ongoing intra-Allied discussions and made a sturdy contribution.

At first I was only a spear-carrier on the conference stage, but after a slow start of frustrating ignorance, boredom, and minor contribution, I then blossomed into the role of starlet. My forte was not the East-West forum as such. At first this required too much cut-and-thrust and analytical skill plus forensic depths of recall about the intricacies of the already long history of the Vienna forum. I became more quickly adept at keeping peace among the NATO representatives themselves by furthering successful compromises in the NATO ambassadors working committee called the Ad Hoc Group (AHG). Compromise was life blood and plasma to the AHG. We had to reach agreement on every word, every comma of three different and often lengthy negotiating documents used weekly in the main East-West meeting. For historically-evolved reasons these meetings were known as the "Informals" and took place around ambassadorial dining room tables where the more learned envoys would often extemporize about past niggling and squiggling, but where the main fare was the reading and noting of three detailed papers on each side. This was, in fact, a far from informal affair since everything was on the record just as much as the weekly plenary speech. Even less "informal" was the structure for the "Informals" — including the exact timing and positioning of the refreshments. These included soft drinks before the session, the host's national confectionery treat half-way through, and a liquor bar at the end which was useful for sometimes-relaxed talk arising from the session. Only once did I notice a rupture in the custom of soft drinks before the session. At an "Informal" held in our dining room the two senior Soviet delegates besought vodka. I gave them two very tall ones since they looked highly hung over. It might also have loosened their tongues. But they were too deep in misery for that.

AHG unanimity was also needed for our bi-weekly plenary speeches, (i.e. alternating with Eastern presentations). Although valuable prior spade work was done in a more junior Western body, the AHG had then to dot the i's — and sometimes the whole alphabet — before the text was finally approved for delivery. And woe to the delegate — and it very occasionally happened — who deviated a little from the sacred text. All this meant hours of wrangling in the AHG, usually much lengthier negotiations than the East-West discussions themselves. Thus the compromiser's role was respected and applauded. Everyone wanted to get home for dinner.

Our delegation had a strong advantage. The AHG discussions were conducted in English only. We were one of the three delegations to gain from this. My UN experience was still relevant. Some instinct for the lighter

The author with his delegation's Military Adviser, Captain (Naval) John Toogood near Vienna, 1981.

touch and a tithe of my father's puckish sense of humour were assets in a jaded group chained to the wheel of consensus. (One solemn European delegate's wife told me that her husband kept telling her about my quips in the AHG. Why did I not make her laugh? What could I say?)

A certain pattern evolved in the AHG in preparing the negotiating papers for the "Informals," the plenary speech texts, and also periodic reports to NATO. Often a left-wing (by NATO standards) delegate would suggest some wording. This would be sharply vetoed by a right-wing delegation. I would suggest a middle formula. The original ambassador would thank me for my well-known efforts to seek compromise solutions but, with regret, he could not accept my wording because it did not meet his strongly-felt concerns of principle. So I would then move the formula a shade to the left. This would still be unacceptable to both sides but finally, as an ulti-mate and great concession, the "left-wing" delegate would accept. The "right" would then usually fall into line through attrition. And another compromise was born. The leftish, *soi-disant,* envoy who usually benefit-ed from these patched-up solutions once asked me if I ever said "No," or did I always respond with a compromise? I belied his snide insinuation soon afterwards by forcing him in the AHG to accept a report to the NATO Council which he had initially opposed. It was the most popular thing I ever did in the group.

The excellent military adviser and deputy head of the Canadian delegation during my last two years in Vienna was John Toogood, a naval captain and expert in arms control. He was a major reason for our useful role. He nicknamed our usual posture and pastime the "Great Canadian Compromise," or GCC. He also ascribed our success to an inherited trait I sometimes employed in the AHG — "the Welsh approach" — a rather tricky and distinctly roundabout approach employed in the Celtic twilight to fox the on-rushing and simple-minded Anglo-Saxons. In the AHG such deviousness worked well. With the GCC and Welsh craftiness how could we lose? It was sometimes fun even if the core of our days was hand-picked ambiguity. (On reflection, I am not quite sure how I can claim Welsh trickiness by blood because my only Welsh parent was about as subtle as a battering ram!)

The duties of the Chairman of the AHG, which rotated among all members including "flankers," required, in fact, occasionally a metallic fist rather than craftiness. I remember two stubborn members seeking to reopen and change a report approved by the group at the previous meeting. In the meanwhile I had become chairman. One envoy was so tough and persistent in his out-of-order request that I finally had to imply strongly that he would be flung out by the chairman if he continued. But on occasion a chairman had to be conciliator. One hot July day when we were in great trouble and travail to finish a text, an impatient ambassador got so annoyed that he told another senior delegate that his proposal was the most stupid idea he had ever heard. The recipient of this brutal blow blandly asked the chairman (me), what I thought of this assertion. In extremis of wits I said it was the sort of unmeant and unintended remark that one might make on a hot July afternoon. That sufficed for the moment. A request for an apology and withdrawal made from the chair in the flame of the moment might have elevated the thing well out of its tempestuous teapot.

Prime Minister Trudeau once asked me, "David, four years of MBFR, how did you stand it?" I pointed out that we operated in Vienna under very broad general instructions with only a rare specific one. Our work of nitpicking detailed texts was by its very nature unsuitable for Ottawa leading strings. I was sure, therefore, that no other Canadian ambassador and delegate had ever spoken up for his country so often with so few instructions. The Vienna talks were also, in themselves, a useful contribution to détente and an East-West channel which could lead eventually to some form of arms control in Europe.

Our Residence in Vienna was historic as well as comfortable. It was one of the Suttingergasse group, a well-known work of an architect, the Viennese Josef Hoffmann. He had been one of a triumvirate of celebrated local architects and designers. They had been European leaders of the Jugendstil/Art Nouveau/Secession movements of the first years of the twentieth century. Josef Hoffmann's stylish work, which included interiors and furniture, was still remembered in Italy and elsewhere. Italian students of architecture arrived periodically at our front door to see the great man's work. If we were not on deck, they sought in vain. Maria, our ex-Polish cook, took no chances. They never got in the door — they were all Red Guard terrorists in her eyes. We took our own chances in the name of art and let them roam about inside.

Maria was a very happy feature of our life in Vienna. We found her after a few months of eccentrics in the kitchen. She was very much a lady in background and shaped like a good cook. She stayed with us for the rest of the route despite being almost brained by a heavy window frame falling on her head from on high.

Despite its pedigree and creator, the house had one large flaw as an entertainment machine. It had One Big Room (OBR). The main part of the downstairs was One Big Room. The owner — the house was only rented — had unwisely created a very large combined living room/dining room by ripping out the wall between them which the good Hoffmann had created. The result was ill-suited for ambassadorial dinner parties. We made do with a screen of golden hue unfolded between the rooms. By candlelight this was effective after stand-up aperitifs in our study upstairs. But the pretence was broken when dinner ended and we herded our guests into the living room portion while the hired waiters removed and clattered away the dishes behind the screen. This procedure was marginally better than taking the guests up the steep stairs again to too few chairs. We eventually took to having large dinners with tables covering the whole OBR, usually with fondue which kept people busy until home time. This we combined with some selective guest swapping between tables to keep the conversational mills going. It went rather well but was not my idea of a diplomatic dinner party mellow with the slow curve of conversation.

The OBR did come into its own as the site of the un-cut-up traditional Canadian reception for "All MBFR." We created this tradition in our first negotiating round and held it on the first night of each Round — the night of the opening plenary. We could just squeeze into the OBR every officer of every delegation. The missing wall was now an asset since social drinking with the socialists was much more fluid and fluent in one big bullring. And the first night of renewed negotiation was potentially fruitful in informal dickering and guarded exchanges since many delegations (not us) had been home since the last round. We occasionally went to the Canadian base in Lahr where we had compressed consults with our Ottawa colleagues who came in by service flight. Tax dollars saved.

East-West socializing had a role in MBFR. Despite the usual rigidity of official stances the informal talk at the functions which crossed the Curtain furnished a useful chance to fly balloons and kites, and to dig, probe, and hint. The crop was interesting but not bumper. The confidences over cocktails and coffee were usually minor key. Even the kites had a short string. Apart from deliberate planting, major revelations were not forthcoming from wary specialists. Even the Poles who seemed designed by nature, or the Soviets, to fly the bluest balloons, never really strayed too far from the ground. East-West fraternizing was not confined to large parties. Duo lunches in mellow Vienna restaurants were regular events, East-West and West-West. The latter nourished cooperation inside the AHG. In order to get a major delegation to agree to a change of AHG meeting time we wanted, I jokingly promised its head a lobster and champagne lunch to demonstrate that the time change would not run us into the lunch hour while giving delegations more time to study draft negotiating papers available only at short notice. It was strictly a joke. Lobster prices were mountain-high in Vienna. But it worked. The time was changed.

To encourage and warm up the negotiations, the Austrian and participating governments used to organize excursions, school outings for deserving negotiators. We made day trips to venerable and attractive towns in adjacent slices of Hungary, Czechoslovakia, and Austria. Our furthest swing was to Holland by Dutch air force. In Amsterdam, Nina had a cordial but hard-punching dinner battle of words beside a canal with the suave but ideologically rigid East German ambassador. A winter foray to an ice-clad abbey in Austria was warmed up when the chilled delegates were filled with Austrian wines in an ancient inn nearby and sent home in melodious buses. The American ambassador, Jock Dean, was always armed with an accordion and quadri-lingual song sheets, while the trained and fulsome voice of the Soviet envoy's wife lifted roof and rafter on every outing — much to the visible embarrassment of her husband. But on our last occasion with them and the Deans, a private dinner in a Yugoslav restaurant in old Vienna, her voice rang out with such charm that an American tourist sought her autograph. Shamed — or perhaps delighted by this recognition — her husband chimed in to her rendition of a Russian folk song.

One other outing calls for notation. The Greek ambassador saved his allowances each year for a major bash — a boat trip with dinner on the Danube for all delegates and spouses. Liberated by water under their wine, the delegates began for once to behave like their forerunners at the Congress of Vienna who wound up the Napoleonic Wars. Dancing broke out and even a touch of indiscretion as we chugged between the high gnarled banks of the river north of Vienna to the castle where Richard the Lionheart was imprisoned for ransom.

The Soviet delegates would sometimes suggest informally that their country and alliance had to be very wary of West German military strength and untrustworthiness. I suggested to a Soviet delegate that this was ridiculous. The German strength was far below Soviet might and they had no nuclear weapons. It reminded me of my old history professor's saying that men and governments were always preoccupied with the danger of the day before yesterday. Ivan thought for a moment and replied, "You may be right but don't forget we had our yesterday — and our day before yesterday" (i.e., the two world wars and German invasions). He implied that this had left strong scars among the older generation including Soviet leaders. "My old mother said to me recently, 'Ivan, I know you have to work with these East Germans but don't trust them, Ivan, don't trust them!'"

In my farewell remarks at my last plenary session — the only time an ambassador speaks his own text not his alliance's — I pointed out that I had not missed a single plenary in four years — devotion or masochism? But I expressed confidence in future negotiations and scattered some good advice. The chairman of the meeting by chance of rote was the Czech envoy who had been a conference colleague since my arrival. He spoke so warmly of my work and persona that I suggested to him afterwards that he might as well have invited me to join the Warsaw Pact. "And why not?" he replied. Little jokes aside, it was possible to maintain civilized social relations verging on guarded friendship with Eastern delegations. One could actually enjoy parties with them, and not just as an extension of information negotiations or boring representational duty. The Russians threw a table-groaning and vodka-soaked reception for all delegates late in each round. The caviar was heaped up in two colours and all was jollity. The chance, the first in our career, to develop some knowledge and some guarded amity with Communist diplomats, was an interesting plus in Vienna.

But what did this cautious conviviality accomplish? What progress did MBFR make in my four years toward its target of agreement on significant cuts in conventional forces in central Europe with a monitored cap and ceiling on all remaining forces? Some progress was made in clarifying differences. More important, constructive work was done on what we called "associated measures." These were concerned with verification and confidence building (e.g., advance notice and monitoring of military manoeuvres by each side). MBFR also provided a continuing channel for East-West dialogue, a channel of general reassurance and aid to détente of wider informal scope than the actual meat of the talks.

A valuable bilateral example of this process was the evolving relationship between the two German delegations. At first they had stayed at frosty baton length but gradually the political gulf was sidelined by the natural warmth of common language, culture, and heritage. By the time I arrived five years later, they were socially closer than any other East and West delegations. But the two Germanies were the root of obstacles to agreement. The large West German forces in the area of proposed reductions, which included the whole of their territory — but no Soviet territory — would be reduced and capped along with the United States and Canadian forces.

This constituted a Western handicap we called the "geographic factor." North American troops and equipment would have to be flown in from long distances in the event of war. Soviet forces could simply surge across their frontiers with Eastern Europe. Their troops in the USSR would not be subject to any constraint. So why did the USSR not strive for agreement? Why did they put forward figures for their armed strength in the treaty area well below the reality known to us? Why did they also block agreement by opposing some verification measures? Their determination to hang on to their Eastern neighbours and, above all, East Germany, was the answer. An overriding factor was the Soviet need to be free to retain and increase at will their very large forces inside those countries in order to maintain congenial régimes in power without facing the serious consequences of breaking a major treaty with NATO powers. This requirement was not met by ability to move in massively after war broke out. Ancient history now, we hope.

Our children were also much at home and happy in Vienna. The German language appealed and gradually soaked in. They enjoyed the sauna and neat little pool in our house. It was also just long enough for me to chug back and forth every day with martini and music at the edge to relieve the tedium of my home-made swimming style. Very good for my disc if not my liver.

By dint of consecutive courses and linguistic elbow grease Nina also acquired a very solid knowledge of German which had to be used up front every day in myriad managerial tasks running our Residence and for incessant representational duties. These included a delightful concert for our conference colleagues in the Residence performed by gifted young Canadians studying the higher reaches of music in the ancient and superb academies of Vienna. At this concert, however, our splendid 1911 Bechstein piano began to emit a few painful noises. This foretold its descent into mediocrity. It seems to have been fifteen years older than we thought. With much regret, especially from the family pianist, Nina, we sold it at a sinfully low price when we left Vienna.

The American International School was vibrant. Caroline blossomed in drama although Michael was thought by some to be more quietly effective as an actor. Both were lively stars of cabarets in the school which were used to extract schillings for charity from proud — or appalled — parents. The AIS teachers were a mixed collation. Luckily the better ones taught in those fields, History, English, and German, which our kids relished. The English teacher was a novelist of calibre and bright imagination, and the Ph.D. historian, a perky but sensitive New Yorker. Some other teachers were awful and the discipline was porous. But the drama director was outstanding and was sufficiently discerning to ask Nina whether I had been a professional actor since the children had so much innate ability on the boards. This muted for a time family criticism of my exploits in charades, a Christmas imperative.

Katherine's surging climb up the education ladder took her from McGill, through Oxford law and a Cambridge first class master's degree in international law, to qualifying as a solicitor in England. She also tutored students at Cambridge. A fellow tutor there had taught me forty years earlier. Her proximity to Vienna was a delight.

Austrians speak their own variety of German with volubility. Some in Vienna speak a local hash or patois called Wienerisch. Our driver did and loved to spill it out. He was proud of being, in effect, trilingual. I decided that a more orthodox German would be of general use to me even though I had no direct official need for it. As noted elsewhere, English was the sole language of the Western group and the East-West negotiating sessions were English and Russian with consecutive translation which was also provided simultaneously in the weekly plenaries. So why learn German — to warm up the distant smattering of it learned in our abortive Bonn posting twenty years before? Daily convenience and cultural interests were the motives. I must have looked like an Austrian, perhaps from the Tyrol. I kept being stopped in the street and asked the way to the Opera House or the Burgtheater or whatever. My attempts to help with the family shopping at the markets were also crippled by linguistic poverty plus a natural tendency to buy rotten fruit — or so my children claimed. I thus took five weeks' training in German in two bites. The kids were then able to flaunt their superiority by cheekily mocking my pronunciation and syntax. But I got by. I could even buy gas as well as dubious fruit and a simple meal, and glean morsels from the television news. My daughter claimed to remember ten years later with vivid horror my fractured chat with the innkeeper of our favourite trail-skiing resort. It was perhaps as well that I was envoy to arms control and not to Austria.

Holidays

Vienna was the hub of the wheel for trips to other European countries. We first ventured to Dubrovnik, in Yugoslavia. This was chiefly memorable for what did not happen en route. Driving moderately on a two-lane highway, we almost hit a horse-drawn hay rick and its venerable driver. He swung right in front of us — clearly not looking through his rear view mirror! Luckily there was a flat shoulder to brake onto. A Yugoslav car pulled up behind us. Speaking German, the driver asked if we were all right. Hearing our rocky reply he switched to English with notably increased warmth. He had been driving behind us and had a clear view of the close call. He walked back to the farmer and poured invective on the man, to judge from his sagging posture. The driver then returned to us and apologized on behalf of the farmer and the Yugoslav nation, etc. The Yugoslav roads are not designed for speedsters. Curve and hill take a toll. After the near hay ride we moderated our pace further. This was no foolish thing. On our way back from Dubrovnik ten days later, three cars passed us on the Dalmatian coast road at notable speed. We subsequently passed two of them — massively wrecked.

The longest and most elaborate of our holiday trips was to a Greek island in the summer of 1979. Through friends in Vienna we rented sight unseen — and unimagined — a house on the island of Alonisos in the Aegean. It belonged to a diplomat, the only one I know of who worked for three governments. Even spies usually confine themselves to two. Our landlord had worked briefly as an Indonesian diplomat after their independence and then as a Dutch diplomat before finally joining the Australian foreign service, apparently because of his Asian expertise. By the time we rented his house, he was Australian ambassador to Brazil!

The house proved more primitive than we had expected — sans refrigerator, sans electricity, sans comfort — but with a sweep of patio poised high above the sea. We forgave the defects. After a three-day drive through Yugoslavia and northern Greece, dodging ramshackle cars of Turkish workers heading home for the August holidays, we spent a delightful day sailing on a car ferry through the northern Greek islands. Arriving late in

The Reece family on a skiing holiday in the Austrian alps, 1980.

the evening in Alonisos, we picked our way in our burdened car across
moon-sized craters on the road to the house. It was in fact two hundred
yards beyond the end of the rocky road. After humping our luggage and
our gear, including an inflatable sailboat, over the stone-ridden path, we
gathered by lamplight, exhausted and enchanted. The caretaker explained
all the features and drawbacks of the place in very fluent Greek. We did
not have a word. But he became our boatman and chugged us to town for
shopping and excellent feta cheese salads under the deep shade of venerable trees in an ancient square on the harbour.

We never had to face up to that pock-faced road again until our reluc-
tant departure. The boatman, Eleftherios, taught us one of the few words
of Greek we needed — it meant Thursday, the day he took us to town by
sea. Our outings always ended in a staggering trip up from the beach and
landing point with chunks of ice for our icebox, the first I had seen since
my father finally and reluctantly sold our last one in 1945 for five dollars.

In late July the beach was almost our private domain. Here we swam in
the warm sea and sailed our inflatable sailing boat. But soon the beach
began to fill with boatloads of bathers from the small hotels in the town.
Standards fell — beginning with the bikini tops. Then one day as I picked
my way down the rocky path toward the beach I felt a presence approaching. I looked up — total frontal nudity. Thereafter I spent more time at the
house reading Trollope.

CHAPTER FOURTEEN

Jamaica and the Western Caribbean
(1982-84)

IN A MAJOR SHIFT of life, job, and hemisphere, I was appointed High Commissioner to Jamaica in 1982, and dually accredited to four other Commonwealth territories in the Western Caribbean. Our three years in Kingston were very full and satisfying. It was an ample assignment. The office was among the ten biggest Canadian diplomatic missions abroad. (There are over a hundred.) This reflected the depth of Canadian interests and the wide net of our ties in the region. The introduction of a visitor's visa requirement in my time brought us another five immigration officers to add to the five handling the regular immigration programs. These included the very useful seasonal worker arrangements which brought six thousand Caribbean workers to Canadian farms each summer, half of them from Jamaica.

Aid had been phased out in Trinidad after our stay there because of oil price rises, but the program in Jamaica rose swiftly because of increased need. The country had been damaged by world price and market trends in bauxite/alumina, aluminum, and traditional agriculture. Tourism had been cut severely by turbulent political violence in the late '70s but it picked up considerably in the early '580s to a rate of about eighty thousand Canadians and close to one million in toto per year. Our aid rose to about $30 million annually before I left. In addition to the tourists who gave us a full range

of consular problems, personal ties between the two countries were extensive through large Jamaican communities, especially in Toronto. To audiences in Jamaica I would sometimes confess that I was wholly unqualified
to represent Canada in Jamaica — audience sucks in surprised breath —
because, unlike everyone else present, I did not have an aunt in Toronto.

Personal security was an unavoidable preoccupation of life in Jamaica.
Political violence had largely disappeared but straight crime was abundant
especially in Kingston. With guards and electronic devices galore we avoid-
ed anything more serious than minor thefts but the medication as well as
the potential disease caused chronic strain. It was an additional reason to
head out to the beautiful beaches and mountains and the lovely countryside in between. Our defences included a bullet-proof car which I used at
night and for VIP visits. It was a handy tool during two days of minor riots
and widespread disturbances in January 1985 — the "petrol riots" —
caused by a sudden hike in the price. We used the "Bullet," as we called it,
to convey Canadian children home from school after trouble began on the
first day. Later, when the driver was on his own, the car proved its invul-
nerable worth. At a road block a small rock bounced harmlessly off the
window but broke the outside driving mirror which was not proofed. This
also badly shredded the driver's nerves.

The unusually high incidence of crime on the island was mainly due to
poverty and desperation plus an inherent taste for criminal violence bred
in appalling slums. Some thefts ended in multiple deaths in order to wipe
out witnesses. This happened to a prominent visiting musician when we
were living in Jamaica.

The police fought back. The press reported quite often that when the
police had apprehended a criminal he was "dead on arrival" at a hospital.
(This became the title of a popular song.) Thinking a touch of informal
diplomacy might be useful, I asked my favourite cabinet minister at lunch
why the police took no prisoners. Slightly nettled, he paused and then said,
"Can you blame them?" I doubt if my slightly veiled criticism did much
good, but economic measures such as the government food stamp program
for the poor seemed a better weapon against crime than "Dead on Arrival."

After a few months in Kingston I realized that the chief desk officer for
foreign aid was, in fact, Prime Minister "Eddy" Seaga who took office in

late 1980 after the lengthy pre-election turmoil. He was profoundly engaged by the deep-rooted economic problems in his country and sought modern solutions. By scheduling regular meetings with him, we were able to cut through stubborn bureaucratic knots in our aid program. His tough shrewd interest provided an extra stimulus and causeway for the program's sturdy growth. At our meetings and elsewhere he displayed a compassion which refuted the widespread belief that his cool brain froze his heart. At a briefing he gave to our visiting National Defence College, I introduced him by noting that he was, of all the leaders I had met on my wide circuit, one of the most concerned for his people. He replied with the quizzical comment that, "No wonder you didn't invite the press here today."

Seaga's policies illustrated a Shavian paradox. His program of short term austerity and structural adjustment according to International Monetary Fund (IMF) precepts was designed to produce a leaner viable economy for the long haul. Suffer now and prosper later. It was clearly the policy of G.B. Shaw's "cold kind heart" as opposed to the "soft cruel heart" which would reject the IMF conditions but suffer ruin further down the road. In foreign policy Seaga was conservative and not just out of deference to the United States which had swiftly inflated its aid program after Seaga's election to about $130 million per annum by 1985.

Seaga had a strong fear of Cubas sprouting everywhere, a legacy in his mind of the former Manley government's flirtation with Castro. Thus Seaga took a lead in Commonwealth Caribbean participation in the United States' invasion of Grenada to overthrow the far left government which had killed the less left Communist Prime Minister Bishop and colleagues. This took me into his office early the morning after the invasion and about half an hour after receiving sizzling instructions from Ottawa to complain that our old friends in the Caribbean involved in the invasion had not consulted us. Seaga apologized quite fervently. One of the other governments concerned was supposed to have told Canada in advance. (This was said in the press to have been the Prime Minister of Dominica and there were jokes about her having lost Trudeau's phone number.) At a later meeting, however, he bluntly turned down my personal suggestion about a possible Commonwealth force to replace the invader's troops. "No way — we'll see the job through!" — and so they did. I had met Prime Minister Bishop at a meeting of all Commonwealth Caribbean leaders in Jamaica in 1982. He was amiable but tense and flanked by conspicuous heavies.

Although cool, dry, and statistical in most speeches, Seaga could be witty. At a Caribbean-Canada dinner at our Residence, Seaga urged the Mulroneys to come often to Jamaica since the other Caribbean islands had grave drawbacks, e.g., Antigua had gone to the Birds (the father and son who headed the government there). I like to think Seaga was also a connoisseur of dry humour. He was very complimentary about a speech I made to an investment conference attended by North American businessmen. Unable to be too enthusiastic about rosy investment prospects in precarious Jamaica, I had garlanded my speech with jokes and anecdotes (e.g., Diefenbaker in Malaya).

I enjoyed the unquenched eloquence of ex-Prime Minister and Opposition Leader Michael Manley during my initial call on him, a ritual appropriate to a new envoy's rounds. Apart from the odd word at social functions and a party political briefing for diplomats, I saw little of Manley at first. Then Manley and I suddenly got on the track, literally. Nina and I got a permit from the local water authorities to walk, run, or stagger on the track around a large reservoir near the university, with a lovely view of the Blue Mountains six thousand feet above Kingston. So we hit the track most weekdays at first light, about 5:30 A.M. Later was too hot. Manley was another regular. He jogged and we walked in the opposite direction — to avoid being hit from behind by jogging zealots. So we greeted him two or three times a morning and had the odd brief chat. During this period we watched a whole cycle of Manley health, two operations and recoveries, jogging cut down to slow ambling and then up to full throttle again.

Jamaica had a high visitor inflow from Canada. Old friends, cabinet ministers, musicians, athletes, boy scouts, businessmen, officials, unofficial delegations, journalists all passed through our door or at least into our garden. The ministers did not stay with us, preferring more space with their assistants and delegations at the nearby hotel. But we entertained them all dutifully and extensively to meet their opposite numbers and stimulate their business. Lunches for thirty or forty spread across the living room which was bigger than the dining room. The two rooms had identical main doors opening on the front verandah. It was thus easy to use one as the other and vice versa. A flexible feeding factory. Oratory in two languages. Once I was challenged by a Jamaican Minister who had lived in Montreal. I seemed to be near the end of a toast to a francophone Canadian minister, Monique Bégin, and had not uttered a word of French. I had, in fact, planned to include a few gracious words but, stung by this assault, I subjected the mainly Jamaican gathering to an impromptu summary in French of the whole speech. Mme Bégin smiled graciously.

Our reigning Minister of Agriculture, Eugene Whelan, paid a major visit in his green stetson. He saw a wide swatch of rural Jamaica, ending up at the extensive farm lands of Alcan. As good corporate citizens, they made fertile use of acreage which was not currently being used for bauxite mining or was reclaimed after mining. Having never seen so many farm animals so quickly in my life before, I noted to the Jamaican Minister of Agriculture's wife as we looked at the back end of a well-endowed bull that I had not realized before how much sex there was in agriculture. Although I spoke loudly, she did not seem to hear me.

On another agricultural occasion, a joint meeting of Canadian and Jamican veterinarians, I was struck by the many references to frozen semen, a valued Canadian export. In my brief and informal remarks I mentioned that this was second "Vets" gathering of the weekend. I had spoken the day before to the Royal Jamaica Legion. I might have added (but luckily did not think of it in time) that in my naval days I had often been wet and very cold — another form of frozen seaman.

After a particularly long meeting when even the vote of thanks was detailed and substantive, a European ambassador asked whether I thought training in the Oxford and Cambridge Unions (student parliaments) was a factor in this Jamaican eloquence. I noted that I had had some experience myself in the Cambridge Union but I had also worked in Africa. I suspected that the speech-making skill in Jamaica had much to do with courteous African eloquence. Most Jamaicans were, of course, of African descent.

Nina and I were once invited to attend a service club dinner meeting on the north coast of the island. The dinner was in honour of a visiting Canadian who held high international office in the same service organization. Nina was to give the prizes. I assumed a few words from me would also be welcomed. After two rounds of drinks at the meeting site with no sign of dinner we grew a little restive — concealed of course. We were then told that unfortunately the chairman was delayed. He should be along soon. After a further delay he arrived with an assistant. Why the latter? To help him carry the hired chairs into the dining room. The prolonged hold-up was explained. A meeting chairman can easily be replaced but not a furniture chairman. Contrary to my expectations, I remained stuck in my hired chair all evening, a very long one. Nina made a charming Lady Bountiful handing out the prizes but the High Commissioner was not asked to speak. I was there as spouse only. Perhaps I should have seized the microphone late in the evening but I was too tired by then to get out of the chairman's chair.

Another piquant public function we attended was the unveiling by Seaga of a statue of the famous Jamaican reggae musician, Bob Marley. The occasion was also a bit tense, and ill-attended by the diplomatic corps. A previous statue had been scorned by the public who had had a look before the planned unveiling. "That ain't our Bob Marley," they cried. The vocal protests of an embryo mob caused Seaga to keep the statue veiled and order a new one. So the ceremony we attended was a successful substitute and the statue a better likeness.

Young musicians from the Canadian National Youth Orchestra played a series of concerts with the Jamaican Symphony and stayed in the Residence. My first chance to carry a cello case, no small thing. The Steinway in our Residence, a joy to Nina's sonata, had a strong pro workout with these keen young Canadians. Nina did not have too much time for the piano. Apart from the house guests, sometimes six at a time, and the whole ponderous entertainment machinery, she took a very active role in voluntary work, mainly through the Jamaica Federation of Women. Basic schools to take care of pre-school-age children were a strong interest. Charity functions run by Canadian and Jamaican women's groups made good use of Residence space and garden. For the first time we had no children with us. Caroline was at boarding school in Toronto and Michael at McGill. But they came roaring down for holidays, often with friends, to the pleasure of our staff despite the extra work. Katherine checked in from London law life as a solicitor — "soliciting on

Katherine, Michael and Caroline in Jamaica, 1983.

Mincing Lane" as I liked to put it. Then she changed firms to one on Cheapside.

Some of our house guests stretched the value of their round fare by staying two or three weeks. Since lounging on our patio and in our pool soon palled, we would ship them off in rented small boats to islands sufficiently far out from Kingston harbour to make swimming palatable. Then we would whip them off to the North Coast which is Jamaica's Eldorado of coves and beaches, endless on the crystal sea. We rented a house nestled in the hills above the sea near the banana port of Port Antonia, a delightful fragment of Georgian Jamaica. After the first house was no longer available for rent, we turned to a more lavish one nearby which was decorated like a Latin American hacienda at the turn of the century and gazed out over a superb view of shore and lagoon. Snorkelling and swimming took over. The latter was a must for my degenerated disc and salt water certainly beats the pants off pools. For the snorkelers the reefs were superb.

Our Residence pool was shaped like a circular plump question mark, just right for an ex-MBFR negotiator. One feature of the pool was its strong and deadly attraction for insects. Being squeamish about hurting or killing any creature and perhaps not totally sceptical about reincarnation, I personally rescued about a thousand insects from liquid graves, mainly bees and flies, who came to drink and stayed to drown. Jamaican wasps, regal

The Canadian Residence, Kingston, Jamaica, 1982.

Old coffee plantation house in Jamaica, base camp for climbing Blue Mountain peak.

and menacing, were far too clever and strong to get sucked in. My well-polished insect-scooping technique also saved the pool bottom from a squishy carpet between hooverings.

Sea and pool would take us through two weeks of long-term guests. For cool relief we sometimes drove them to a weekend house near the Kiplingesque army training base of Newcastle carved out of the hillside at four thousand feet above Kingston by an enterprising British major-general. He guessed that its cool air would prevent yellow fever which had previously mowed down U.K. troops in Jamaica. Understandably, he became a field marshal.

Appetites whetted by this brief tang of cold nights and bright clear days, our hardier guests were then shifted to the base camp in the Blue Mountains about three hours' drive away. The road, almost vertical in places, led through hill villages to a haunted house in on old coffee estate with a distant view of the sea. The coffee was still abundant but we never saw the "duppy" (ghost) said to haunt this classic eighteenth century fore-man's dwelling. Its fireplace was a roaring asset in the evening. Its lack of electricity took us back to the ice box age. The household would move upwards at 5:00 A.M. to climb Blue Mountain Peak at 7,400 feet. This required a struggle up a winding path from the house at four thousand feet, the same height as Newcastle but with many a valley in between. It was a stiff walk through rain forest of exquisite beauty, sharp sun and the whack of sudden wet clouds. When it is occasionally clear you can see halfway around the island from the peak — although not to Cuba as the fanciful claim. Going down, even junior knees creaked.

To accompany successive waves of house guests, I climbed the peak five times. And could never find anyone in Jamaica who could match my boast-ing — they had all peaked too few. Finally my prowess was recognized. The aid section of our office recommended that we give ten thousand dol-lars to the Jamaican hiking and trail authorities to develop paths, build huts, etc. for this useful alternative mode of tourism in a country where tourists were the second biggest dollar earner. Always groping for a quip, I suggested, in jest, to the officer responsible that in return for that much money from our small project fund the Jamaicans should name a trail after me. So they did. Many a wise word said in jest. I trust that my colleague's

*Nina and David in the Alcan alumina plant, Jamaica. Mr. and Mrs. Garrard from the
Canadian High Commission also present.*

mistake of one for the other will not lead to future charges that I used public funds to buy myself a winding monument in the Jamaican hills!

Although trade with Jamaica was hobbled by its foreign exchange dol-
drums, the Canadian commercial profile was high in the country. Alcan
had two large bauxite mining areas and alumina plants (the intermediate
stage before the high-energy smelting of aluminum). Three of Canada's
bank chains were highly active, two of them the largest bankers on the
island. Other companies made periodic forays seeking investment and
trade openings. One firm asked me to arrange a dinner with two local journalists so that a relaxed and ranging discussion of Jamaica's future could
take place. Knowing journalists, I invited three. Only one turned up and
he was very late. He was also at the outer edge of sobriety. He asked for a
large whisky and his coherence level sank. I rushed the small group to the
table and urged bread on the journalist. Luckily he ate all courses heartily
and clarity was restored. In fact, he saved the evening by then providing a
brilliant tour-de-Jamaica which the Canadian guests valued. In diplomatic life swift injections of food are sometimes salutary. At a large dinner in
the Residence for a visiting Canadian VIP, the wife of a fellow ambassador

showed distinct signs of much drink taken. Luckily she sat beside me at table. As her head bobbed up and down and threatened to sink onto the table, I plied her with bread and the meal. This became known in the family as "Daddy's bread-stuffing act." In this case the absorbent worked so well that she was seen to drink abundant cognac after dinner and still leave head high.

Functions at the house were not all large dinners, lunches, or receptions. At regular intervals I had tête-à-tête lunches with an amiable cabinet minister who would pass on gossip and insights in return for my own views. I would lunch the over-worked official head of the foreign ministry. This saved him office time and the minor infusions of relaxing liquid made the discussions more fruitful to both sides. Aid teams and External Affairs officials — known to us as "snow birds" when they flocked down in winter — benefited from large and small lunches for shop talk with Jamaicans. Businessmen and trade groups were hosted with local counterparts. The presence in our kitchen of a stately genius, coached and directed by Nina, earned us a high gastronomic rating and an enviable guest acceptance ratio. The number of return invitations was low. Diplomats do not expect to be invited back except to official functions where the local government or firm pays the tab. Guests know that the diplomat uses his ministry's funds, not his own. Thus not many private Jamaicans returned hospitality. One exception was the family Irvine; he a brilliant doctor and his wife a warm and charming *materfamilias*. Ronald Irvine had been a cabinet minister but had resigned over a policy difference grounded in government fiscal aridity. But he and Cilla knew Tout Jamaica and their parties were a delight. Another couple, Desmond and Peggy Blades, provided warm hospitality on water, picnics and swimming from their boat. EEC representative Roger Booth and wife Karen spent weekends with us by sea and hillside; our friendship endures.

Our neighbours, the Chinese, built a tall concrete wall between us known to us, of course, as the Great Wall. It was part of a general security policy and stretched to other neighbour perimeters. Incidentally it stopped our respective dogs from quarrelling loudly at the former wire fence. At that time, the Chinese ambassador, who was short of English, had one stock bit of business he used to trot out. "Canada and China are good

friends. China-Canada dogs not good friends." I used to say that my answer
to the Wall was the Chinese water torture (i.e., I tortured the Chinese with
my classical records played loud and clear so that I could enjoy them over
the splashing of my daily swim).

Other neighbours posed a delicate problem. They were a delightful
young couple and good friends — once we solved the barnyard problem.
This was a crowded duckpond with adjacent hennery located on the edge
of their garden and just below our bedroom windows — but not their bedroom windows which were on the other side of their large house. We
enjoyed looking out on this happy quacking scene of domestic duckery on
our first day. But next day our pleasure flew away on the crow of a very
vocal cock. He started up at about 4:30 A.M. and shattered our light sleep.
He quickly became a big bane. Our neighbours pointed out that the cock
was the special gift of a Jamaican cabinet minister who would be upset if
it were returned or eaten. I sent the neighbours a letter citing a line from
Hamlet, act V. This was the line, "The rest is silence" — Hamlet's dying
words. When Shakespeare failed, I said I would tell the minister our problem and ask him to relieve our adjacent friends of this burden. That finally did it. The rooster was shifted to a point equidistant from the two master bedrooms. When the neighbours left several months later, a friendly
successor disposed of the fowl. So ended the "Great Cock War." Amusing
in retrospect.

Our one naval visit came twice — in a sense. A Canadian Navy sailing
ship used for training had to cancel its scheduled arrival at very short
notice because of mainmast troubles. We thus gave a phantom ship party.
It was too late to cancel the reception arranged for them. The local guests
included carefully culled young women who found themselves in a pout-
ing majority with no sailors to meet. But when the ship eventually did
make it to Kingston a few weeks later on its way home, we were not able
to make it up to our charming friends. The crew and trainees on the ship
had undergone a sea change. They were now mainly young women sailors.
We now had to rustle up a squad of young men. Daughter Caroline, who
was spending the summer working with the children at the S.O.S. village
for abandoned youngsters, was helpful in this new selection process. She
had friends in the younger ranks of the Jamaica Defence Force. Its alche-

my worked. From abandoned children to abandoned behaviour! The party, with bodies and chairs in the pool, also starred a weeping male seadog who broke down into his birthday cake. All this and Jamaican reggae, strident calypso and very big hard rock went on to the edge of dawn. The Chinese must indeed have been tortured. We were left with a reminder of this happy occasion. Our new kitten was named after the lachrymose seaman.

An even more important event was the visit of Prime Minister and Mrs. Mulroney in late February 1985 for a two-day meeting with Caribbean heads of government in Kingston. This was of course the climax of our posting. I take a little lefthanded credit for the birth of this happening. Some months before the Canadian election of September 1984, I had suggested to Mr. Seaga, without instructions, that he might like to visit Ottawa after a Commonwealth Finance Ministers' meeting in Toronto in September 1984 unless there was an autumn election in Canada. One was in fact called for September 4th but Mr. Seaga is a determined man and eventually received an invitation to pay a quick visit to the new Prime Minister. He needed all his stubborn will to keep this date because his plane developed engine trouble. He was thus only able to see Prime Minister Mulroney for twenty minutes because the latter had to dash off to receive the Queen arriving in Ottawa. But some rapport was struck in that time and the Kingston meeting inseminated.

This gathering of the Caribbean clan went well, good chemistry. Emphasis was on reducing or removing residual trade barriers in Canada and our Prime Minister renewed an aid-doubling pledge made originally by Prime Minister Trudeau at a meeting in St. Lucia I had attended. (I had been unusually silent then because I was feeling ill; I was not amused when I was subsequently told I had made a very good impression at the meeting.) The Caribbean Prime Ministers were relieved to hear our renewed pledge. They were afraid that it might have been torpedoed by the new government's concern about an inherited budget deficit of groaning dimension. Certainly it was a heavy concern. On our way to Kingston from the airport the Prime Minister dwelt on the problem. I mentioned Jamaica's similar concern which Seaga then underlined at a bilateral meeting.

The kick-off for the conference was a large Jamaican government reception. Since Seaga and wife Mitzi were anchored to the receiving line as

Prime Minister Seaga of Jamaica, Prime Minister Mulroney and Reece, Kingston, Jamaica, at a bilateral meeting before the Canadian Commonwealth Caribbean leaders' meeting in 1985.

hosts, he suggested I take Mulroney and Mila around to meet the other Caribbean leaders. Thanks to my past and present dual accreditations and attendance at conferences in the area I knew most of the major guests. Some of them had lost and then regained office since I was in Trinidad, a healthy working of the democratic process. Mulroney was the hit of the night. A good kick-off for the conference.

In addition to our aid pledge, the Kingston meeting underlined the importance attached to Canadian relationships, especially appreciated because they were free of the big-brother heavy breathing sometimes linked to U.S. connections.

Social events at the conference were important for informal talks and getting to know the new boy. At a buffet lunch hosted by Seaga I was at a table of six, the only one present who was not a Prime Minister. Mr. Mulroney was the star while the leaders of four Caribbean states, small but genuine parliamentary democracies, and all with a good knowledge of

David with Sir Florizel Glasspole, Governor General of Jamaica, and Lady Glasspole at the Canadian Residence, Jamaica, 1984.

Canada, pumped our Prime Minister for insights into his massive election victory. I kept my mouth shut.

The social crown of the conference was a dinner in our Residence with twenty-seven heads of government and chiefs of apt multilateral agencies including Commonwealth Secretary General Ramphal. This galaxy neatly fitted into a line of tables running the length of our living room. Before we got to it stress and travail naturally bobbed up. Just as the first guests, the Seagas, arrived all forms of electricity cut out — stoves, refrigerators, lights, air conditioning. It looked like a long, hot, dusky evening. Distinguished government potentates cannoned into each other in the dark until all the contingency candles were lit. After much hostly fret our head servant found the button of the auxiliary generator in the pitch-dark garden. The automatic system had failed to work; I had been close to giving up. But now all went as merrily as a Caribbean feast. Our Prime Minister said he and Mila were official hosts but this was a legal fiction. Nina and I were the real hosts who had made all the arrangements. He then graciously toasted us.

Nina had indeed worked very hard with the Ottawa supply people to supplement our dining equipment. The meal was a concerto of culinary skill which required much advance orchestration. My major role was, as usual, the table plan, which stretched to the limit this first skill of my diplomatic youth. My father used to call Canadian football trench warfare mixed with higher mathematics. Table plan making is arithmetic mixed with tact. The problems this time called on the latter more than the former because the rules of precedence were hazy. Do you put Ramphal over the Premier of Bermuda? Yes, was my decision and no one looked vexed at other protocol judgements in the ranking of the leaders of states in different stages on the ladder to full independence vis-à-vis the heads of various international agencies.

The successful conference had a swift and unhappy sequel. A week later the Prime Minister of Barbados, Tom Adams, died of a heart attack after playing a prominent and witty role at the Kingston meeting.

Nina and I starred in our own pale light in August of 1985 at the Governor-General's customary lunch for departing envoys (i.e., us this time). Sir Florizel Glasspole was a delightful, courteous, and vigorous older man who much enjoyed company. At the lunch he described Nina as a charming badger with her stripe of white hair across the dark brown. He also made some agreeable comments about myself and the visiting Reece daughters who were at the table. But when he turned to Katherine's chair it was empty. She was urgently engaged in a stomach upset in the Government House gardens near the dining room which was mercifully open at one end. This enabled her to make a discreet exit before the moment of truth which was watched by an unfriendly alsatian. Misère! But she made a gallant comeback in time to say goodbye to the hosts with mendacious murmurs about stomach flu. In fact, the Minister of Culture, who sat with us and with beakers of cognac in our garden after our farewell dinner the night before, had something to do with it.

PRIME MINISTER FOOTNOTE: Brian Mulroney was not the only Canadian Prime Minister to visit Jamaica in my time. Pierre Trudeau paid an annual holiday visit with his three sons. They stayed with old friends on the North Coast. During his first two visits he was in his last stage as Prime Minister. I duly met him and convoyed him to his holiday site, once by car and once in a helicopter. Like courtesies were provided on his departure by the chargé d'affaires in my absence from Jamaica. The second visit was in the last few weeks of his long reign. When I expressed regret at his imminent departure, he thanked me but said it was time to go. "And the boys think so, too. Don't you boys?" A short silence was broken by the youngest, Michel. "Yeah, you know, I've been asking the kids at school what it's like to be an ordinary kid — and they say it's kinda nice!"

What do you do with an ex-Prime Minister when he arrives for the same holiday as usual? Do you provide the same courtesies as for his last two visits when he was Prime Minister? A Great Canadian Compromise was necessary. An officer, who was up on the North Coast for the weekend, met the Trudeaus and I saw them off at Kingston airport two weeks later. Trudeau had shed years in appearance. When his plane departure was delayed, he courteously insisted that the Jamaican Chief of Protocol and I should not wait with him. It was a Saturday evening. I never got around to asking Michel whether, as forecast, he enjoyed being an ordinary kid. I expect so.

Belize

In the eyes of constricted islanders Belize seemed a gently rolling plain stretching forever. It was one of our two major dual accreditations in the area. With a land size several times that of Jamaica, Belize has only a thin skin of population, 150,000 to Jamaica's 2.2 million. Belizeans are agreeably mixed: African, Mayan, and other Amerindian plus whites of diverse origin. These included at least one American we knew, Emory King. As a young man he had intended to sail around the world but got shipwrecked on Belize and married a lovely local girl of Spanish descent. His business waxed in various directions and he became the Honorary Commercial Representative for Canada. He and our Canadian Honorary Consul, Linda Gordon, who had married a Belizean and worked for a CIDA project, ensured with kindness and efficiency that our ten or so official visits to Belize were "sixty seconds worth of distance run" for each minute there.

At least one-third of Belizeans lived in Belize City. It is an appealing scruffy town of twisting canals, jaunty battered wooden Louisiana-style houses with slightly sagging balconies and outside staircases. It was the capital until a few years ago when the periodic ravage of hurricane and flood persuaded the colonial authorities to shift the seat of government inland to Belmopan not long before independence in 1981. This pleasant new town has Mayan-style office buildings set in a green wilderness fifty miles or so from Belize City. It still looked like a golf course in search of players. The large green areas were dotted with signs announcing the future presence of such and such embassy. One of the very few already there is the British High Commission, naturally. The U.K. retained the former Governor's residence for their envoy until his own was built, while the Belizean Governor-General made do in a crowded suburban house.

We had two centres of involvement during our well-packed visits. The Prime Minister and his cabinet colleagues worked in Belmopan in modest ministries. There was no hotel there. An attractive new one was under long construction. Our major aid project was in Belize City and the headquarters of the government authority concerned was also there along with businesses and banks, including Canadian. So we divided our time. I found the city of Belize all too full of signs about Canada. They marked the main sites of our CIDA project, a new water and sewerage system. (Note the difference between sewage and sewerage, the product and the process.) So far this consisted of torn up streets and large urban holes. Whenever a street was blocked and traffic diverted, one saw a red maple leaf! We had other small economic development projects scattered around the country from our small projects fund controlled by our office in Kingston, not Ottawa. One of these, a "Breast is Best" centre, was regularly visited by our towering CIDA officer, an experienced family man.

Much of our dealing with the government in Belize centred on these projects. The ministers were grass-roots and pleasant to deal with. Their officials were competent and forthcoming. Since Belmopan had no hotel we lunched them at a sprightly open-to-the-air restaurant with name to match, "The Bullfrog." The Prime Minister was generous with lunches at a small government guest house. Belize style was the reverse of lavish. Senior civil servants passed around the meat and vegetables. This modest tone reflected the first Prime Minister after independence who had been Premier and Chief Minister for some years before that. George Price is a shrewd but simple man. He lost the first post-independence election in 1984 and transferred power with swift grace. He won it back at the next election. Before the 1984 elections in both countries we had Canada's first ever ministerial visit to Belize. Roy MacLaren, Minister of State (Finance) and his wife Lee were enthusiastic and friendly VIPs who went down very well with the Belizeans. I arranged to host a dinner for MacLaren with Price and his colleagues which drew forth good talk and anecdote. One minister seemed preoccupied but this is probably pure hindsight. He ended up in an American jail fairly soon afterwards, caught in an alleged marijuana export "sting."

The government arranged a press conference for MacLaren. My doubts about the fertility of this had comic confirmation. In addition to the government press officer the only others present were a journalist who concentrated on the drinks provided and a rather fierce young chap in a wool cap who revealed a sharp left slant. He asked if Canada planned to control Belize through our sewerage project just as the U.S. had held Cuba to ransom before the war through American control of the Havana water supply. The Minister's reply was suitably dry and sour.

A more swinging feature of the visit was an archeological probe. We drove to the northern area of Belize with the MacLarens, to the fragrantly titled town of Orange Walk. From there we boated in convoy, a police boat bristling with hardware ahead of us. This was not mere courtesy or super caution. There had been recent violence in the area from border incursions and perturbation in refugee settlements from neighbouring Central American countries. (A Guatemala claim to much of Belize had resulted in retention of important U.K. deterrent forces there.) At the end of this winding trip we were greeted and lunched and enlightened by an admirable pair of Canadian archeologists, the David Pendergasts. They lived with their small son in a simple, breeze-cooled Mayan-style house amid important and large-scale Mayan ruins. In showing us their work, including a unique giant stone face and a fascinating collection of artifacts, they revealed themselves as highly skilled and intelligent practitioners of a demanding and uncomfortable profession. Dr. Pendergast and his father had both made major contributions to Belize archaeology at other major sites. The link with Canada was also nourished by training provided in Canadian universities. The Acting Director of Archeology at the time of our trip up-river was a charming young Belizean woman who had trained at Trent University.

Bahamas
An advantage of dual accreditation is access. Scarcity value as a visitor and the more modest dimension of the country enable you to call on heads of state or government, cabinet ministers, and senior officials, more easily than is often the case in your country of residence. There they usually

expect you to have a special reason or VIP visitor in order to take the time of the mighty.

Bahamas was no exception. I called on the Prime Minister, Sir Lynden Pindling, on some of my visits there, three or four times annually. We talked of bilateral relations including trade and tourism and problems of the Caribbean and the Commonwealth as a whole. Relations with the U.S. were a shade strained at that time. This may have sweetened my access. Pindling, a political veteran, was host to a Commonwealth Caribbean summit in my time and a Commonwealth summit soon afterwards (in October 1985). Both were creditable successes. When I called, Pindling was always patient under questioning and frank in reply. His bright and articulate woman Cabinet Secretary was a helpful interlocuteur as were a variety of ministers, especially on trade, transport, and tourism, questions of mutual concern. We have no aid to Bahamas — too much per capita income — but Canadian tourism was a big slice of bilateral relations, about 100,000 people a year. The Bahamians thought air links should be strengthened to swell this figure. Our trade was livelier than with struggling Jamaica but the distances involved in contrast to U.S. exports were a major obstacle to increased imports from Canada. Our banks were very active and provided confidential offshore banking. I saw their local chiefs in Bahamas and Cayman.

Nina and I also enjoyed calls on the Governor-General, Sir Gerald Cash, a gentlemanly, cheery lawyer who was a relaxed and considerate host. He combined discretion with generalized candour in our discussions. His traditional white-sided and gun-girt Residence was perched up on a mild hill in Nassau.

Two successive Honorary Consuls were a great help to us and their sharp secretary a jewel. The tourist flow with problem spin-offs kept them very busy. Honorary was a fictitious title.

Nassau, the Bahamas capital, was fate fulfilled for me. Most of my childhood was spent in a house on Nassau Street in Winnipeg. The southern Nassau is a bustling elegant little city which spreads out along the ocean front and across a toll causeway onto the so-called Paradise Island. This Valhalla is populated by large new hotels and a major casino. Paradise for winners. In the centre of town the older white classical buildings and stone churches are under perennial siege from tourists. Many are day trippers from the cruise ships which are a permanent but shifting backdrop to the Nassau waterfront.

Bahamas confronts the tourism Catch-22. The very success of its major income source, tourism, threatens future expansion by overcrowding beach, street, hotel, and even casino thus deterring additional visitors. The government has sought escape from this noose by building an enormous yellow hunk of hotel on a good beach well out of Nassau and equipped it with its own casino and abundant conference space. (I claim to have vanquished the Nassau casinos by ending twenty-five dollars up on the voracious fruit machines.) Another hope for bigger and better tourism is the plethora of delightful smaller islands in the Bahamas galaxy. Time straits stopped us from seeing them.

Turks and Caicos

Grand Turk was the site of my only all-woman banquet. I felt like a pasha. The hostesses were the Soroptimists of this island which houses the Turks and Caicos colony capital, Cockburn Town (a good candidate for a Trivial Pursuits question). Nina and I were being fêted in a new day care centre which had been built and equipped by these women with a good lacing of our small-projects fund for these islands. At the dinner I was outnumbered thirty to one, a good ratio. A small Turk at least.

Grand Turk is in fact neither grand nor Turkish. It is a literally low-profile island of former salt-making pans (or ponds). It smelled at times like Ottawa in the heyday of paper plants in Hull across the river — "And when the wind is in the East, the fumes will curl your liver." (The punchline of a ditty about Ottawa which I once wrote.) But in Grand Turk lovely bare beaches, pellucid sea, and excellent deep diving usually filled such sturdy inns as the Saltraker.

Turks and Caicos is still a colony. The Governor was a brisk and dedicated Englishman who rode his job and his official limousine, a converted London taxi, with jaunty concern for his parishioners. With strong Whitehall support he fought hard and with some success against the drug transit trade, which used airports and strips in the colony.

Turks and Caicos caught attention in Canada a decade before my dual accreditation there. Their then Chief Minister and his majority party favoured some form of union with Canada. This was to provide a southern warm spot in return for financial flows from the north. A few Canadian members of Parliament supported this imaginative idea which sank on the rocks of practicality. During my first visit to Grand Turk I received a call from a leading figure in the now opposition party which had supported the union when in power. He told me his party had whittled down this plank from merger to new and stronger ties. My office was in fact already fertilizing such links through our small-project funds. Our efforts were aided by an able and assiduous Briton under contract to the Turks and Caicos government as their development officer. He was a cornucopia of proposed projects. There was only one Canadian bank with one branch in the colony but plans were afoot to develop confidential banking à la Cayman.

Tourists were relatively few but there was some spasmodic Canadian interest in hotel ownership. With a total population of about eight thousand the islands benefited from even a tourist trickle. The main target for the trade was Providenciales Island, more hilly and attractive than Grand Turk, home of a new Club Méditerranée nourished by a U.K.-funded airport. On the tiny Salt Cay near Grand Turk a brilliant American architect was slowly creating a small hotel to employ rather than combat and despoil nature. He was building a complex of salt box reproductions on the beach.

Cayman

Like Turks and Caicos, this mini-responsibility called for an annual visit only. Still a British colony, it consists of two little islands west of Jamaica with fifteen thousand residents existing comfortably on a healthy flow of tourists and a concentration of offshore confidential banking. Canadian banks were big. As in Bahamas, I always called on their head men and discussed banking problems with ministers and officials including the Governor.

Cayman was less evolved constitutionally than Turks and Caicos. This was by their own choice, apparently based on a desire for legal buttress and protection. There were no official parties in Cayman although elections were held based on the rivalry of informal groupings stemming from family ties. There was neither cabinet nor ministers. Instead they were called members of the Legislature for Agriculture, etc. The executive power was in the Council chaired by the Governor and included three senior officials. One was from the U.K., the Attorney General. In foreign policy and defence the Governor had primary power locally but with reference to London, whom he also consulted about using his power of veto in the Council in other spheres (e.g., finance). This apron string set-up suited Cayman despite all its ties with North America and in fact partly as a counter balance to them. As a former student of colonial history, I found this rare living fossil of early constitutional development a fascinating case study.

Since the turtle production of Cayman had been severely crimped by American import restrictions, inshore shrimperies had become important. On my last trip I learned of a new and ocular development. A breeder had doubled the size of the shrimps in his pond by blinding them in infancy through laser surgery developed on humans with the opposite objective. This appeared to be the latest word in scientific barbarism but it has been pointed out to me that this process, which is apparently used by other crustacean farmers, causes its subjects to live happier lives. Their added weight is the result of being spared the stress of seeing the complex anxious problems in the world around them!

Cayman is crawling with condominiums and seaside villas. Since I had barely heard of the colony before, I was rather startled to find a sizable clutch of compatriots in full or partial residence. Benevolent tax arrangements are as much a reason, I suspect, as benevolent southern breezes. We met many of the Canadians at receptions kindly hosted by the governor and his wife. His official car was much grander than an ex-taxi.

CHAPTER FIFTEEN

Ottawa, Zambia and Malawi
(1985-90)

THIS HOME POSTING began like the year of the locust. We came back to Ottawa after a seven year stretch to face heavy expenses of house repair and education. A senior job, which I was expected to handle for the next three years, did not materialize. I hacked away at three short assignments. At least Michael and Caroline were only short hours away by road and train at their universities. I eventually acquired a responsible and interesting job, heading a task force to organize and administer a meeting of NATO Foreign Ministers in Halifax in May 1986. The locust cloud had lifted.

It sounds rather simple, but organizing a successful meeting to take place hundreds of miles away in collaboration with the NATO Secretariat thousands of miles away is not that easy. Happily the Nova Scotia government pitched in with great enthusiasm from the top down. Premier John Buchanan and his protocol and conference centre chiefs were models of positive cooperation and energy. The NATO civil servants concerned, under a redoubtable Turk, knew every rope. My own task force was built up gradually. It contained only one other but deeply experienced External Affairs man on a part-time basis. The rest were a patchwork of contract and agency players who pulled well together.

I subsequently became a senior policy advisor on arms control — a throwback to Vienna days. Then I was appointed High Commissioner to

Zambia and Malawi in 1987, a final stretch in Africa, and a logical finale to a career largely devoted to Commonwealth developing countries. With bright visions of wildlife dancing in their heads — a fantasy soon made flesh — our children, now in their twenties, approved this posting with vigour and planned their visits. When they came, sometimes with friends, we had a gamut of game trips and many piquant views of endangered species — lions, leopards, rhinos, and elephants, and a wide range of other creatures from the bizarre beauty of giraffes to grunting and scurrying wart hogs. Nina and our children endured with fortitude rafting down the Zambesi River below Victoria Falls the magnificent. I did not join them. Over-sixties not wanted on this voyage.

The climate of Lusaka is superb. Spread on a limestone plateau of 4,200 feet — the height of the hill stations in Jamaica — Lusaka had only one really hot month per year despite its relative proximity to the equator. The Lusaka rainy season is also a gentlemanly affair with few real drenchers. The year we arrived it had been too restrained (i.e., a middling drought).

The Residence was unattractive but well suited to official entertaining. Our lawn was croquetable. The games were intense but sadly intermittent. Only the Reece children were up to H.E.'s lofty level on the pitch.

When posted to Zambia we had enquired about the Residence piano. Non-existent. So let us get one of those modest but serviceable Japanese models which we had obtained for the Ghana and Trinidad Residences. It was clearly our destiny to make music in previously silent embassies. But no dice this time. No money available for such things. But ten minutes later the administrator who had given me the bad news called back after a little head scratching and told me there was in fact a Residence piano stored in Rome after the Consulate General in Bordeaux had closed down. It soon winged off to Lusaka. It proved to be a splendid Steinway baby grand. We embraced it with zeal and harmony. It was the focus of charity concerts in our Residence and a continuing delight to both occupants and guests.

Lusaka living had one severe negative: insecurity and the reasons for it. Theft was frequent in Lusaka although its authors were not usually professional. (Except for car thieves who fed an insatiable market in Zaire.) Basic need and hunger were the usual motives and few thieves carried guns. I strongly discouraged Canadians, CIDA, and High Commission staff from joining armed vigilante groups. If you start shooting, innocent bystanders can be hit. I therefore persuaded Ottawa to stump up a hefty ongoing sum for a security company which provided an instant response team in a jeep with clubs not guns. They arrived a few minutes after the householder pushed a button. These teams were strategically stationed in different parts of town. The system was very effective and necessary. Police transport was usually lacking in suburban stations. Various break-ins, including one in our house, were aborted without bloodshed thanks to these teams plus piercing alarm sirens, motion detectors, guards at the gate, and razor wire on high walls. But our Residence had been thoroughly robbed earlier in our stay when we were in Malawi. An officer's gardener had been killed before the new system was in place. Stern high fences were almost *de rigueur* in our suburb and diluted the pleasure of my daily walks. I would see only the roofs of sprawling bungalows, the style favoured in Lusaka. Compensation on my strolls was provided by troupes of Zambian kids who called out bird song greetings and shook hands with solemnity. One felt like a benign Pied Piper.

A foreign service joke is sometimes applied to Lusaka. According to this, the traditional retirement post for an aging ambassador is a civilized and amiable European capital awash with cultural amenities and not much work for the envoy who thus slides gently into retirement. The other type of retirement post such as Lusaka makes you want to retire immediately! But the joke is unfair to the Zambia post despite its security hazards. Nor does it provide a gentle slide into superannuation. There is, in fact, a great deal of work for the Canadian mission and its boss to do, much of it of considerable worth and interest. Some of this was in the wider field of African affairs. Zambia's President, Kenneth Kaunda, was a leader of high stature in the international arena. In 1987 he was elected head of the Organization for African Unity for the second time, a rarity. He made valiant attempts and some progress toward solutions of various intra-African disputes. We were kept well informed of this subject by senior Zambians. Kaunda was also permanent head of the Front Line States (FLS) which border South Africa and have suffered the damage of destabilizing activities by the apartheid régimes. The African National Congress (ANC) was fully based in Lusaka for most of my posting. It was a favourite target for Pretoria's security forces. We kept in regular touch with ANC leaders who also became an important source of briefing for visiting Canadian VIPs including Joe Clark.

Clark was the able and firm chairman of a Commonwealth continuing committee of nine foreign ministers which met every six months and did a valuable job of focussing and intensifying attention on apartheid and measures against it. The committee's first meeting was held in Lusaka in February 1988. The low key but highly intelligent Zambian foreign minister, Luke Mwananshiku, was a valuable member. (His friendliness and intricate surname encouraged one to use his first name!)

Giant strides toward the death of apartheid began with President de Klerk's assumption of office. President Kaunda met de Klerk just before he took office. Soon after this meeting near Victoria Falls in Zambia Kaunda told me at a function that he judged the new South African leader to be a good and honest man — "But will he have enough time?" The verdict is still awaited.

The next great step was of course de Klerk's release of Nelson Mandela in February 1990. Appropriately his first trip was to Lusaka where a boisterous and surging crowd and Front Line States, OAU, and other leaders including Joe Clark paid tribute. Mandela's courtesy of manner and the moderation of his views were almost astonishing against the background of his decades in prison and detention.

Zambia's stature was also reflected and exerted in Commonwealth meetings where Kaunda worked closely with successive Canadian Prime Ministers. Their cooperation was notably effective in efforts against apartheid and in warming bilateral relations. Kaunda's respected position as a Commonwealth veteran and the Canadian site for the 1987 Heads of Government meeting (initialled CHOGM and pronounced with a choking sound) led me to a modest triumph which almost became a quasi-comic disaster. I hosted a lunch for Kaunda before his trip to the meeting. The other Commonwealth envoys in Lusaka were non-paying co-hosts. Kaunda was clearly pleased and said it was the first time such a courteous and appropriate occasion had been arranged for him before a CHOGM.

His warmth might have cooled, however, if I had not pulled back from the very edge of the abyss in my toast to him. A curious "time-gaposis" attacked me. Although we had left Ghana eleven years before, I came within a slender sibilant of toasting the president of that country instead of Zambia. After a brief but agonizing-for-me pause I came out with the right country. In practice, however, Kaunda might have been more amused than incensed if I had said Ghana instead of Zambia. He would probably have made a joke of it — and never have let me forget it. This happened to a mild gag of mine at a ceremony opening an important Canadian aid project. Kaunda and I were the main speakers. I noted that in this company I really felt for the first time like a "High Commissioner — a very High Commissioner." Thereafter when we met — and he was very accessible to envoys and visitors — he would often ask me solicitously whether I was feeling very high or low, etc., and then explain the joke to anyone else present. I guess I had asked for it.

Kaunda's geniality and love of pleasantries were on daily display. They were ingredients in his most important gift to Zambia — his work for national unity in a country which was in desperate need of it — a country of sprawling dimension containing seventy-three tribes and languages. When we were there it seemed to have achieved a viable identity. Part of the price was the need for educated Zambians to work and be schooled in a second and very different language, English. At the beginning of every speech Kaunda cried out — in English — "One Zambia — One Nation." His own contribution to this was monumental.

Our daughter Caroline, who made six visits to Zambia during our posting there, including a few months working for UNICEF, was very familiar with Kaunda's national unity cry. Too much so. Back in Canada she accompanied me to a big dinner for Kaunda who was the main speaker at an international AIDS conference in Montreal in June 1989. When Kaunda gathered his delegation together after dinner to sing the Zambian togetherness ("Pamodzi") song, he began as usual with "One Zambia — One Nation." But Caroline was half a syllable ahead of him in the second half of the slogan. Her voice was not subdued. Kaunda spotted us and asked us to come up and join the Zambians in their song. This was fine for Caroline but I cannot sing a note. And the next night at the Canadian government state dinner in Ottawa for Kaunda he assembled his Zambian colleagues again and then demanded that "my High Commissioner in Lusaka" come up and join in the Pamodzi song. I subsequently assured my companions at the small head table, including the Mulroneys, that I had adorned the front row of choirs since I was a sweet little boy and had always obeyed instructions to open my mouth but never let a sound emerge.

At a very small dinner for Kaunda in Montreal given by Ivan Head, president of the International Development Research Centre and chief organizer of the AIDS conference, I warned Kaunda that Caroline, whom Head had kindly included, had just finished a course of African studies at university. She therefore knew all about Africa. Kaunda should thus be careful what he said. He chuckled at this pleasantry and was very amiable in answering Caroline's points and questions. There are not many heads of government on whom you can lay such a cheeky attempt at a joke and get away with it. But I knew I was home free in this case.

Kaunda was different from many leaders in Africa — and elsewhere. He led a one-party state but its human rights record was better — much better — than in some countries, including neighbours. Although the media were government controlled and the President was elected in one-party contests, press and parliamentary criticism of government activities — but not its leaders — was lively. Demands that Kaunda retire were reported, as were facts and allegations embarrassing to Zambia's rulers. At a coup attempt trial in 1989-90 it was alleged by the defence that Kaunda had billions of personal dollars stashed in foreign banks. This received banner headline treatment in one Lusaka daily. Political detainees were held without trial but their numbers were limited and their detentions subject to judicial review at regular intervals. In July 1990, a few weeks after riots and looting followed food price increases, Kaunda released most political detainees and the jailed looters and rioters. This was part of a "love not hate" campaign. Characteristically Kaunda hosted breakfast with each of the different groups of detainees (except the looters) just before their release. One had been the leader of a 1980 coup attempt whose description of sleeping on the concrete floor in "death row" for four years was given front page prominence in the press. Others released included the senior army officers whose coup attempt in 1988 had been aborted by an informer. Their trial was abandoned.

These improvements in human rights and clemency were followed after my departure by an implemented commitment to a multiparty system and the end of power monopoly by UNIP, the government party. In 1991 Kaunda and UNIP lost heavily in general elections. He left office graciously and an impressive government has succeeded him, including two of my friends in Lusaka.

These steps toward a liberal democracy are naturally congenial to Canada as a Commonwealth comrade and economic partner. Our aid to Zambia was vigorous, but shortly before my arrival in Lusaka in 1987 Canada had decided not to make any new aid commitments to Zambia for the time being because Kaunda had abandoned a structural adjustment program for its economy favoured by the IMF, the World Bank, and major donors. However, despite this no new aid policy — and in an act of benign contradiction which I had strongly advocated at high level — Canada wiped out Zambia's bilateral aid debt to us *in toto* (86.3 million dollars). We also had decided to make all future aid grants, not loans. This was sensible. Why create debts which can never be paid by a poor country which needs every scrap of capital and foreign exchange for building its economy? Our wise decisions, which were applied to other Commonwealth and Francophone aid recipients, helped to create positive deliberations at the Vancouver CHOGM. It would have been unwise to single Zambia out as an exception to the debt wipeout when Kaunda had naturally to play a key role in the anti-apartheid consensus at the imminent CHOGM. Canada, as host of the CHOGM, had a major stake in its success.

New Canadian food aid to Zambia was then promised despite our policy of no other new aid commitments there. Along with previously committed large packets of food and rail freight cars, our total aid in my first year or two was ironically higher than it had ever been. This included ongoing projects in agriculture such as the development of new wheat seeds. These overcame hostile elements in the soil of north Zambia and grew without irrigation which was rarely available in that region and certainly not to the small farmers the project was primarily intended to benefit. We targeted agriculture as our core of aid concentration since Zambia's future must lie there. We also had projects to build roads for farmers and to aid the agriculture faculty of the university and government economic planning. Zambia's copper output, still the source of most of its foreign

The author visiting CIDA road project in northern Zambia, 1987.

exchange, is dwindling sharply in this decade as uneconomic pits close. To find the resources needed for this drastic reshaping, Zambia returned to a policy of structural adjustment in 1989. The consequent new flow of foreign exchange included Canadian balance-of-payment support badly needed for the transition period.

A small and unusual but very effective aid project took the form of a Canadian Governor of the Zambian central bank. Jacques Boussières was on loan from the Bank of Canada for two or three years financed by CIDA. He was an immediate inflow of non-stop energy and wisdom in the directing corridors of Zambia's economy. He was at home and skilled in international conference work. This was of vital importance in his job. Aid donor conferences were key elements in winning resources essential to Zambian growth. A cheerful workaholic, Boussières earned high respect through expertise allied with tact in dealing with colleagues who knew that he was the first foreign governor of the Bank of Zambia in twenty-six years of independence. He even endured weird and wonderful Zambian pronunciations of his name. I felt guilty there. Kaunda had phoned to alert me shortly before his public announcement of Boussières' appointment.

With President Kenneth Kaunda of Zambia, 1987.

I should have given the president a tactful lesson in French pronunciation.

Walter McLean, MP, came quite often to Zambia in his capacity as the vigorous Special Canadian Representative to Africa and the Commonwealth. On one of his sorties he led Canadian Parliamentary observers to Namibia with a side visit to Lusaka. During a lunch discussion they had with ANC leaders, a prominent Communist ANC leader urged the continued need for force. The members of Parliament were clearly not convinced.

On another visit McLean led the Canadian delegation to a regional economic meeting where donors were welcome and appropriate participants. His skill as a golfer was also considerable. On one visit he played a round with a Zambian golfer of high calibre, President Kaunda. Since my golf was below par for this assignment, I walked around with the players but not just for the walk. On the eighth tee I asked Kaunda to support Canada's bid for United Nations Security Council membership. At the nineteenth hole (i.e., at lunch after the game), he delivered Zambia's vote. Green grass diplomacy.

Kaunda was open and generous with time for visitors. He loved to follow a business meeting with a working lunch where the visitor could have useful dialogue. Working breakfasts and dinners were also common. The latter ritual included the presidential host himself dishing out the coffee afterwards. This disconcerted some overawed visitors. The evening meal was usually at 6:00 P.M. This was a blessing to me on one occasion, an informal conference at my office and Residence of four Canadian ambassadors from the region with two Ottawa officials. We had been allotted an afternoon meeting with the president. Because of this I scheduled our large official dinner for my colleagues for 8:00 P.M. Then, at short notice, Kaunda kindly decided the afternoon meeting would be followed by a working dinner. One could not say no but only pray for the usual snappy meal in State House and for double appetite! As we left after the meal one of the guests for our own dinner, Kaunda's economic advisor, almost danced with mirth as he said goodbye to us. But we made it with five minutes to spare and manfully handled our second three-course dinner.

Another large dinner we gave for a party of senior Canadian officials had an even more enlightening effect. We had been suffering for some weeks in our Residence from frequent power cuts without warning or pattern. The cuts were caused by serious fire damage to the power facilities at the Kariba Dam. Candles were kept handy at numerous strategic points in our large house. No big sweat — especially as it was not a very hot time of year. But most of the districts around us had fewer or no cuts. I wrote an official letter of polite remonstrance to high authority. Nothing happened.

Then came the dinner which was attended by two Zambian cabinet ministers. The percentage of turner-uppers compared to accepters was unusually high. All went merry as a diplomatic dinner until the big cut came as usual without warning. I was secretly delighted as the candles glowed and the gas oven became the instant focal point for a large meal. My pleasure was based on a hunch. Sure enough, both ministers went to the telephone in rotation. A few minutes later the power surged on. So ended unfair discrimination. We never had another cut. Disgraceful use of ministerial power? No. Rectification of a wrong by a happy chance. One of my colleagues was succinct. If a letter does not work, try a minister!

Because of distance and a severe Zambian shortage of convertible cash our exports to that country were mainly aid not trade. However, a rare and sizeable trade package was shaping up before I left in August 1990. This entailed various calls on ministers and officials to sell instead of give, since there were rivals in the field.

We had earlier hosted an impressively expert group of Canadian specialists in mining equipment and accompanied them to the Copper Belt where their main hope for sales lay. The only resident Canadian enterprise of any size was the ubiquitous Bata Shoe under a very capable Canadian manager in Lusaka. We were able to help him when unfair government pressure threatened Bata's future in Zambia where their miner's boots were especially useful. I had two chats with the main cabinet ministers concerned and thus helped to make the shoe pinch less. Bata stayed.

Colleagues

Our office was slender in human resources but my two senior colleagues made up for our small numbers. They were both richly experienced and nimble officials. Bob Pim, a talented and flexible officer, headed our aid team. His cheerful persona and well-honed ability to get on with third world people and problems made him a formidable operator.

Gerry Ohlsen, who managed our trade, economic, political, consular, and immigration programs was a vigorous man of robust good cheer. He was adept at solving practical problems but he was also the author of shrewd and lucid telegram reports and memos. His lively spirit of camaraderie enabled him to mingle fruitfully with all sorts in all conditions. He and his wife had long since taken on a unique and loving commitment, four children of different races adopted in Ethiopia and Guyana. In Zambia they added one to the vivacious team, a very small boy they originally sheltered for health care but found ungiveupable. They adopted him.

Nina made her own very well-directed input into the Zambian economy. She patiently shaped up and honed small projects for Catholic schools, clinics, and rural hospitals, etc., and then persuaded foreign aid agencies and NGO donors to help pay for them, including the foreign exchange needed for equipment. Before she took it over with verve, the Catholics had no one to do this vital work at the grassroots. The church's gratitude was of matching importance. The Pope gave her a medal. I teased Nina that as a Canadian humanist with roots in the Orange Lodge married to a Canadian envoy she had a lot of nerve accepting a decoration for working

Farewell lunch in Lusaka for Nina given by the wives of the Prime Minister and Cabinet Ministers in August, 1990.

for a foreign power (i.e., the Vatican and its local envoy, the Papal Nuncio). And I had not even been able to accept a Ghanaian medal for saving a technical college from night soil! But this time the Canadian government could hardly have been so mean spirited as to say no to the decoration or the job — if we had bothered to tell them. Nina also worked on a committee of diplomatic wives and Zambian women to raise funds for a mothers' shelter at the huge hospital in Lusaka.

When Caroline was not visiting Zambia she was at the University of Toronto for a B.A. and then at the University of Ottawa for a diploma in development studies. A French course at the University of Montreal led to joint authorship of and acting in a sprightly play in French about the disastrous efforts of a Canadian embassy in the aid field. (No, not her father's embassy!) Caroline used her summers to travel around the U.K. as a tour guide for good pay. This helped her decide that she would like to be a career guide (i.e., a school teacher). Her enthusiasm and warm sympathy should be assets here.

Michael had three trips to Zambia and visited with zest game parks in Zambia, Botswana, and Malawi. He joined other guests in turbulent rafting of the Zambesi rapids. Michael's post-graduate career was more practical than academic — working in a kibbutz in Israel and a Club Med in

St. Lucia. The latter included an introduction — and farewell — to trapeze artistry. Too tough on the shoulders! Michael's summers were a mélange of tree planting and supervising young campers in Algonquin Park. This latter experience, his humour, and his simpatico personality have led him also to the teaching profession.

Katherine spent three Christmases in Zambia, Zimbabwe, Botswana, and Malawi. She, Nina, and Caroline made an epic trip on their own to south Malawi by jeep when Nina opened a Salvation Army project funded from Canada. Katherine's legal friends joined our charades and our safaris.

Malawi

A country of fresh beauty with a magnificent lake, green fields intensively cultivated, and twisting hills, Malawi is a seriously crowded terrain with one-fifth of Zambia's land area and about the same population, eight million. This means meagre plots and farms. Malawi's per-capita income remains near the bottom of the world scale. This is unlikely to change while its population growth remains at its current rate. Fortunately their government was relatively efficient and well-organized. I had regular evidence of this in my calls on various ministers and senior officials during my visits to Malawi every two or three months. In Malawi too I called often on resident envoys to fill in the gaps since my last visit. They were usually happy to tell all to "a barefoot boy from out of town." As in West Africa there was much to tell which was censored from the press.

The frustrations of directing an aid program in Malawi by telephone and telex plus short visits were mercifully reduced after my first year in Lusaka by the appointment of a middle-ranking CIDA officer to run a two-person sub-office in Lilongwe, Malawi's smart new capital, much of it built with South African loans and investment. Our officer there, Steve Hallihan, who reported to me, proved top grade in efficient hustle. Our aid program was modest. Malawi was not a country of aid concentration but a small program can entail almost as much work as a big one which has larger but perhaps no more numerous helpings. The bureaucratic manoeuvres can thus be of similar volume. Our Malawi program concentrated inevitably on agriculture. Farming, some of it the efficient production of cash crops and agro-industry, plus fishing in the great lake, are the staples of a country without marketable minerals. Fertilizer, paper for education, and a useful dairy project were our main aid instruments but we had also built an attractive Natural Resources College. By the long arm of overseas coincidence its architect was my Ottawa neighbour, Pat Murray. It was built before I came on the scene but I paid an official visit, replete with speeches, to its impressive buildings, facilities, and curriculum.

My calls in Malawi were sometimes on President Banda. These usually took place in his favoured residence, a palace perched on a hillside outside the old commercial capital of Blantyre. He was always alone in the vast cabinet room except for a stuffed lioness beside the long table and a leopard's head snarling at us from close range on the table top. Banda was a victory over time. Like Kaunda he led the independence movement in his country, served a stretch of detention under the British, and played a leading role in the demise of the Central African Federation dominated by white Rhodesians. But his leadership began much later in life than Kaunda's. Banda was thought to be ninety or more when I last saw him. A man still effectively in charge, he once summoned me at very short notice to Blantyre to discuss a delicate aid matter.

When I got to the airport for my flight to Lilongwe and onward journey back to Lusaka, I found the flight cancelled with no explanation and no notice. I felt for the only time in Africa the cold breath of danger when I learned later that the plane had disappeared on a charter flight early that morning. While travelling on the usual route to northern Malawi it had been shot down by Mozambican anti-aircraft guns as it made the regular overpass of their territory. The route was immediately changed for all future flights to an all-Malawi voyage. Meanwhile I drove to Lilongwe with a hired car and driver of untested merit in the swift dusk along the road which is the border with Mozambique for eighty-five kilometres and occasionally the scene of border forays by the rebels in Mozambique. But I was well used to travelling this road in my own car which I usually brought over from Lusaka. My preference for road travel was now reinforced.

The charter plane crash, which killed all ten occupants, was not intended. The gunners thought it was a rebel plane. The tragedy was ironic because Malawi's relations with Mozambique were improving. This was true of its relations with the other Front Line States despite Malawi's strong and unique ties with South Africa. These were based on Banda's sense of acquisitive pragmatism. Capital, trade, and tourism were valuable results of not being a Front Line State. At the same time Banda told me he had been the first to crack the ice of apartheid. During a state visit to Pretoria in 1970 he had threatened to leave immediately if he was not allowed to host a multi-racial dinner of reciprocity at the end of the program. The South African state dinner had been whites-only save for Malawians. The host government reluctantly gave way.

In the late 1980s Malawi had begun to play a bigger role in attempts to end the civil war in Mozambique. This was an important and expanding problem for Malawi. In 1990, there were an estimated 800,000 Mozambican refugees in Malawi according to the United Nations High Commissioner for Refugees office in Lilongwe. The strain on Malawi infrastructure and land in a crowded country was heavy and growing. The international agencies, to which Canada contributed heftily, provided the basic refugee living costs, but the social strain from and on poor and crowded Malawians living in the regions of main refugee concentration in southern and eastern Malawi was increasing. Despite this burden Malawi accepted all refugees from Mozambique and forced none to go back. This humanitarian policy is cited as some offset to the trenchant criticism for Dr. Banda's human rights record and social policies, made by respected groups such as Amnesty International and Africa Watch. They have pointed to the tightly curbed media, unwarranted and unreviewed detentions, and stern measures against opposition groups.

During my last year in Zambia and Malawi an interesting experiment in aid responsibility began. A regional aid office (officially entitled a CIDA decentralized office) began work in Harare, capital of Zimbabwe. Its relations with my office and aid program were still evolving when I left the scene but the basic scenario was to move decision making to the field. The regional office was a chunk of Ottawa detached and based regionally to speed things up. Many decisions which posts had sought from Ottawa would now be made by the regional bosses. Major programs and projects would still be settled in Ottawa with recommendations from post and region.

Before this major shift of decisions was launched I had strongly underlined the need to retain management of the aid program (i.e., local leadership) in the hands of the High Commissioner. Otherwise his knowl-edge would be slighted, his local standing damaged, and his valuable access to top Zambians and Malawians unused. I therefore opposed with success some of the initial draft plan. Our cooperation with the regional office in the important initial months was enhanced by the two senior officers there concerned with aid to Zambia and Malawi, Diane Spearman and Jean Perlin. They were intelligent, versatile, and experienced.

CHAPTER SIXTEEN

Diplomacy

THE TITLE MAY be ominous but this chapter is not an essay on the art and craft of diplomats, anymore than this book is a textbook. There are two popular views on diplomacy I would like to mention. One maintains that it is a very expensive and wasteful commodity. I agree — in a sense. Countries rich and poor maintain embassies which quite often do not earn their keep on a daily basis. Much multilateral diplomacy is very labour intensive and often provides meagre returns for great effort. But I would suggest that diplomacy, acting for the political will, does pay its way over the long haul in hard results from such fields as trade, aid, immigration, international law, and environment protection. In the international political field the case is easy to make. The ultimate penalty for failure in arms control and international security would be death to the earth.

Another view is that embassies are supine and passive messenger boys deprived of real influence by modern telecommunications. Ambassadors merely obey orders. This thesis forgets that instructions are often sought by embassies and influenced by their views. Embassies also argue against and oppose instructions. Sometimes it is more fruitful to give a local twist in acting on them, a constructive gloss. The capital need not know — or at least not until after the event.

On one occasion I was asked to arrange a visit by a Canadian candidate for an important international office, who was seeking support. But the country where I was resident and accredited had its own worthy candidate. They would surely be angered by an apparent attempt to obtain his withdrawal or to rob him of votes from his own region. The visit was finally and mercifully cancelled after an escalating series of telegrams to Ottawa from our embassy which finally won the agreement of the Under-Secretary.

Sometimes embassies have to act without instructions because there is no time to get them — or the embassy prefers to play it that way. Often instructions are superfluous. In one third world country a senior visiting Canadian executive turned down an offer from a local businessman to buy the company's local branch plant. He was threatened with instant arrest by the disgruntled would-be buyer who had high-placed influence. I got rather angry at a seemingly childish spat but one tinged with ominous chill. (My annoyance was partly based on disappointment at this real life drama causing me to miss my daughter Katherine's amateur play.) I told the local businessman that I would go to the head of government immediately if there was any move toward arrest.

The next morning at the airport I was ready to act strenuously if there was any attempt to stop the Canadian executive from leaving the country, but the plane was six hours late. I took him back to the Residence and provided soothing gins. His local agent was sufficiently concerned that he phoned their factory to see if it had been occupied by the authorities. It had not been and was not. But I still accompanied the much relieved Canadian to his plane and felt a sharp twinge of pleasure at his clear exit. And I had been able to see the third act of my daughter's play the night before.

Diplomatic Life

Diplomacy is a career that absorbs more of life than most jobs. It is not 9:00 to 5:00. It spills into meal hours and evenings of unpaid overtime. It can inflate the waist line and erode both sincerity and the liver. "But think of all the countries and people you meet ...." Free tourism in depth. True, but there is a price. You never stay long enough to make enduring friends. The locals know that diplomats are hardly worth knowing. They always leave in a year or two. You rarely serve twice in the same place. I was lucky. I had two tours in India and was able to pick up a few Indian friendships I have hung onto — but this is exceptional. You may serve twice with the same diplomat, Canadian or foreign, but this too is exceptional. Three times together is mathematically very unlikely but it happened to me once. In a fifteen-year stretch I served in the same capital with a Dutch diplomat three times. He was younger but had become an ambassador in our third posting together. He and his wife were very successful. At a farewell dinner we gave them I noted in my toast to them that he was shaping up quite well under my third-time tuition.

What does all this do to your private life, apart from shortening its hours? In our case it means that our good friends are nearly all ones we made at school, at college, or within our extended families. What does it do to your children? They have the chance to acquire wide knowledge, perhaps wisdom, and certainly languages. They meet all sorts and conditions in foreign and sometimes exotic lands. They do make lasting friendships and keep in touch amazingly. Changes of venue and schooling are sometimes in fact no more frequent for diplomatic families than for others who move around in Canada in their jobs. And External has over the years improved the directives and financial provisions re family life considerably in such fields as boarding schools and travel. Our children benefited from this enlightenment by the time they reached their late teens, when it matters. Oddly enough, when Nina researched the question of teenagers in diplomatic families, she found them to feel least at home in Ottawa. Abroad they belong in schools catering to a majority of foreign students, while in Ottawa they often cannot break into high school cliques.

Foreign service families have varying fortunes. For instance, the Reeces must be front runners for the dubious prize of outward mobility in our foreign service. In the nine-year stretch from July 1969 to June 1978 we lived in seven cities (Delhi, New York, Quebec, Port-of-Spain, Accra, Ottawa, and Vienna). Our children seem to have survived well this intensive rotation but one of them when asked if the foreign service would appeal as a career replied, "No thanks, Dad, I've seen it." None of them has joined up.

All jobs are different but foreign service is inevitably rather special. Is it worth it? I found it so but some do not. They quit early or wish they had. But in terms of job satisfaction and worth many find foreign service hard to beat. It is certainly better than selling soap or cigarettes. The service is sometimes futile or of very limited scope and significance, boring, and petty. But at other times you feel that you are making a contribution to a tangible and useful step in international relations, that you are making a difference. Who can ask for more?

Diplomatic Day

At a student meeting in Toronto in 1985 I was asked to recount a day in the life of an ambassador. I complied but time was too short. This is an attempt at improvement. My Jamaica posting is the model.

In Jamaica we started early — 8:00 A.M. I began by looking though the telegraph traffic by then available from our gallant communicators who came in earlier. This included copies of outgoing messages. I had approved the important ones the day before but a little mental brush-up was helpful. The routine ones had gone out from the heads of section but repaid a glance to keep abreast of the ten different programs that I was supposed to be managing with hands on or off — or hovering.

It was then a good time to draft reports to Ottawa, in encoded telegrams. They were all aimed at being cost effective (i.e., concise and helpful to various bureaux in Ottawa). These included economic decision makers such as CIDA, the Finance Department, and the economic and trade captains in External Affairs, to whom Jamaican economic health was of direct interest. I shared the general reporting duties with the Economic/Political Counsellor. Being the boss, I could and did assign myself whatever subjects I liked, but in practice the counsellor tended to draft more of our economic reports including a long and detailed quarterly analysis. Other heads of section consulted me about important reports.

The average diplomatic report is a pastiche. The elements are official reports and other public material as background, private views of ministers, diplomats, and officials perhaps culled the night before at a social function, confidential views handed over in offices, telephone chats, and lunch discussions. Material from journalists which cannot be used publicly for some reason is included without attribution. These are second-hand goods but the fresh ingredients come from the observations, discernment, and analysis of the embassy scribes. They may also throw in a little cautious forecasting.

Dictating a telegraphic report and other correspondence before getting bogged down in phone calls and meetings had clear advantages. Whatever the report's contents — factual with initial comments on Canadian interests, or a more portentous analysis of changes in government policy, or the likelihood of domestic political upheaval, or the reply of the Jamaican authorities to some *démarche* we made with or without instructions — whatever the contents and flavour I showed the draft to the other officers concerned and heeded their suggested improvements. I was a shamelessly facile word-slinger. I used to dictate the more straightforward or urgent telegrams in final form.

After the morning reports I had a brief meeting with the Political/Economic Counsellor who acted as chief of staff for some areas (i.e., defence relations, consular, and public affairs). Three times a week I met the head of the aid section who administered a lively and growing program. Once a week I met the heads of the other programs (i.e., immigration, trade, administration, health and welfare, CSIS, and police liaison). I was also in touch with them often in addition to these scheduled meetings, especially in the case of immigration and administration. A full scale meeting of the Committee on Post Management (CPM), composed of all program managers, was held at least once a month to consider major questions of administration. This forum sometimes produced tedious exchanges about matters outside the range and direct interest of the protagonists but this inevitable steam-letting was healthy. The open discussion of administrative snarls and mysteries jacked up the quality of our management. A subsidiary committee on housing with spouse participation was good for management and morale. As chief of mission, I was the major beneficiary. Support for the administrative officer was sharply increased by the CPM's full-scale participation in management. Program heads and their staff — and their spouses who had a major stake — lived more easily with decisions they had helped to shape.

Every month or two there was a separate meeting to decide on small aid projects in our area. The aid, trade, and political heads attended to provide a broad-based consensus. I chaired the CPM and aid meetings. I did not operate on the basis of Lincoln's cabinet (one vote from the chairman is enough for a majority in a crunch even if all else vote no). But there were

a few occasions when the weight of decision had to rest on me alone as
High Commissioner.

After the morning meetings the balance of the office day was a variety
show of phone calls, a high level local enquiry about a visa, an urgent
Ottawa enquiry about a short-notice visit to Jamaica, approval of telegrams
and letters and rewriting of some, ad hoc office discussions and phone
calls, and visitors, private or official from Canada (e.g. a senior bank or
Alcan executive or a CIDA official, consultant, or delegation). Some
Canadian youth group or voluntary organization representative might
drop in for a briefing. I might call on the Foreign Minister (with or without
instructions) or some other minister or senior official or the Prime Minister
for one of our regular aid reviews or to discuss Caribbean affairs (Grenada).
This sort of timetable would, of course, be thrust aside if there was a
Canadian VIP in town when I would be hooked into his/her program.

In the later afternoon there were sometimes ceremonies concerned with
our aid projects usually requiring a few words from me or just a smile at
the camera. Public meetings are a favourite sport in Jamaica. Ambassadors
are always in demand. I used to carp about our role as three-dimensional
wallpaper but these appearances were sometimes useful for occasioning a
quiet word with a VIP, as well as for flag flying. And you can always shut
off your mental hearing aid until the tenth agenda item or so, the Vote of
Thanks, a blessed event. And then, of course, there are those splendid
meetings where you yourself are a speaker, or even the star. Official meals
and receptions were all too frequent items on the program. They are discussed separately.

Diplomatic Reports
Whether aimed at trade, political, economic, or various functional
bureaux, reports to Ottawa, usually telegraphic, carry a standard distribu-
tion in most cases. This may include very senior officials but not normally as action addresses. They are information addresses. Who does what
about any action required is determined in Ottawa. Occasionally — in my
experience very occasionally — a report is addressed to the Under-
Secretary alone asking that his heavy weight be thrown into the ring in support of the telegram's author. I have only resorted to this upper-channel

weapon twice that I can recall. It worked each time. Keep your powder dry. If you go to the higher levels directly and too often, you will annoy the working ranks below.

I have never sent a personal report or plea to the cabinet level. But I have received a report from a Prime Minister. During Prime Minister Trudeau's holiday visit to Jamaica in 1983, Prime Minister Seaga invited the Trudeau family to go boating. The two families were staying not far apart on the North Coast. Having passed on the invitation and made some simple arrangements for the outing I thought my humble role was done. It was, therefore, a pleasant surprise when Trudeau phoned me from his holiday house. It had not just been fun in a boat. The two fathers had discussed affairs of state, a natural opportunity created by the adroit Jamaican. Prime Minister Trudeau gave me a succinct report of their talk among the rigging. I passed this on to Ottawa as expected. I refrained from gilding the lily.

My only other direct and personal report from on high — leaving aside ministerial visits to one's post — was much less agreeable. On this occasion, my phone in Ottawa rang early in the day and our minister for External Affairs gave me a brief but vigorous blast. In a memorandum to him I had provided an escape clause in our compliance with an international resolution on United Nations sanctions. This clause had not been made sufficiently plain in my memorandum. It had been included at the determined request of the trade and economic bureau concerned. I was upset the more when I found that our economic people had been called first by the minister and had, without warning me, passed the buck to me as coordinator and drafter. Forewarned I might have more effectively soothed the high-placed irritation.

Aggrieved and with icy memories of trudging blocks in sub-zero weather to attend various meetings on the subject I wrote a memo to the minister's office. This is a way of by-passing the ironclad procedural step ladder for memos to the minister himself. My memo to his office outlined in detail the thinking behind our proposed compliance with the international requirement and also the exigencies of the deadline. His office showed this to the minister. He returned it to me expressing understanding and appreciation.

Diplomatic Corps

I was amused to hear an ambassadorial colleague compare the quality of diplomatic corps in the two countries to which he had been accredited in recent years. He did so in quasi-culinary terms like the texture of a soufflé or the blending of a salad dressing. Because they are herded together at functions of many kinds, ambassadors see quite a lot of each other perforce. At a Remembrance Day wreath-laying in Lusaka I found myself standing beside the Soviet ambassador waiting for a ceremony to begin. It was the day after Canada had become world hockey champions. I slyly but very courteously congratulated the ambassador on the excellent performance of the Soviet team which we had defeated in the finals. If Canada had not had the advantage of home ice and the games had been played in the Soviet Union, I was sure the Russians would have won. The ambassador gave me a cold look and informed me he knew nothing about ice hockey. Chess was his game. Game, set and match to the Soviet Union. Despite this cool overture we became quite good pals as the ambassador opened up in a Western direction, reflecting his government. During one long chat with him at a dinner party I was amused to find that the IMF had a Soviet friend in Lusaka. In an outward and visible sign of rapprochement the Canadian and Soviet envoys agreed to a joint party of farewell from the corps, two old codgers going into retirement.

Diplomatic Doyen

He is the most senior ambassador (i.e., been there longest). Apart from giving farewell parties to colleagues, which were quite numerous in large corps, the doyen was the corps' contact with the local government on such matters as diplomatic privileges and security. I do not recall this ever doing much good. One doyen delighted in summoning meetings of the corps which were all the more tedious because he did not speak the local international tongue and thus his ponderous remarks had to be translated. Another aging ambassador — I forget whether he was the doyen — had a dinner party for his own first secretary. The only other guest was another ambassador. The host demanded that the other envoy stop sleeping with the young first secretary's wife. A gallant and unusual démarche but I do not believe it stopped this species of *esprit de corps*.

Diplomatic Lunches

Apart from the obvious lunches on demand for visiting Canadians, I found that the most fruitful — for head not stomach — lunches were what I called "four squares," namely the U.S., U.K., Australian, and Canadian colleagues. I initiated these in one or two posts but I first got the idea from an American diplomat in Malaya who had a lunch circle of first and second secretaries. At whatever level shared knowledge and confidences were savoured.

For the above reason Commonwealth envoy lunches were in my experience preferable without any local officials attending. Confidences about the local scene were then feasible. Because of the Commonwealth's size it was sometimes necessary to initiate a general discussion before sitting down to the meal. There were too many lunchers to have such discussions conveniently at a long table.

The way to have senior officials and cabinet ministers to lunch was alone, with one colleague from the Canadian office to help steer the topics and help with recollection and reports afterwards. One-on-one seemed in any case a bit too cosy and thus inhibiting. In one capital where foreign exchange and luxuries were scarce Nina arranged to serve the same delicacy dish to the foreign office head every time he came to lunch after he enthused over it the first time. I am sure he considered this a courtesy not a bribe.

Diplomatic Receptions

I have been to all too many. In fact I estimate that including official functions of all kinds I have put in about five years of unpaid overtime in my career. Many consider receptions frivolous and wasteful use of the tax dollar. I cannot maintain that the practical return for every diplomatic party equals the financial outlay. But for the diplomat — and banker, industrialist, lawyer, doctor, college professor, whoever — such parties provide a chance for an informal and relaxed discussion with someone of value, someone difficult to tackle cold on the telephone or call on officially to discuss the matter. Parties are also, of course, a bazaar for garnering topical views which can be woven into reports. Despite its lingering reputation for formal stuffiness, diplomacy thrives best on informal nuance and relaxed subtlety.

Receptions are also useful if you have a group of Canadian visitors to entertain and provide contacts for. For example, we twice had visits from participants and directors of the National Defence College during our time in Jamaica. At our receptions they hopefully learned something from talking to a variety of Jamaicans including opposition members and the Governor-General. They were thus rather like National Day parties but with more point to them. In fact, ironically, our two receptions for the NDC finally decided us against giving any more National Day affairs. Better to have functionally and specifically oriented receptions. National Day parties tend inevitably to be pro forma and stereotyped turn-outs of fellow diplomats, perhaps one cabinet minister and a few officials plus thirsty nondescripts recruited to fill out a respectable number. In our case the U.S. National Day three days after our own tended to overshadow it. Better to use the available accountable allowance, which in our case was not earmarked for any specific type of entertainment, for more useful aims.

I do not think our fellow envoys noticed our six-year stretch in Jamaica and Zambia without a National Day party. We continued to attend theirs in the hope of useful conversations and to show our flag. Too often the third world countries tend to blow their yearly allowance or much of it on this one lavish party in the most expensive hotel available and then notably fail to entertain usefully for the rest of the year.

Diplomatic Drinks
In Jamaica five or six of the principal aid donors used to meet monthly after 5:00 P.M. for what we called a "working scotch." This was an excellent clearing house for aid news and intentions, and helped avert overlap. In Zambia this proved hard to regulate because of the large number of donors, but we arranged some useful informal and ad hoc sessions for core donors in our Residence.

Diplomatic Dinners
In most capitals there is an expectation that diplomatic dinners will be topped off with a genial toast to the guest of honour or the guests in general. At a dinner I gave at the Residence with seven Jamaican government ministers present I used an adaptation of a John F. Kennedy joke in my

toast to the guest of honour, a brilliant CIDA Vice-President, Keith Bezanson, who had previously urged me not to venture this risky ploy. Filled, however, with the success of this high octane dinner, I threw the dice with abandon. I began the toast by thanking the guests; this great turnout of VIPs was a tribute to Bezanson and CIDA. Never before had there been in this room such a concentration of intelligence, experience, political ability, acumen, sagacity, and wit since the last time Michael Manley dined here alone. (He was Leader of the Opposition at that point.) There was a short gasp and then a great roar of laughter. Despite the bitterness of their political wars Jamaicans love a joke.

At dinners hosted in various capitals I rubbed or conjured up pleasantries within the mellow afterglow of a good dinner rendered more palatable than otherwise. At a dinner in Africa for a senior cabinet minister who had just been appointed an ambassador, I was, I thought, more sparkling than my wont, comparing the parallel skills between diplomacy and ministerial tasks. I knew the minister quite well. He had once helped me to obtain an important decision from his government in a very sensitive matter. I certainly owed him a dinner. Without referring to the confidential assistance he had rendered, I gave him a warm welcome to diplomacy and its servants.

He replied graciously. He noted to my amused surprise that he was delighted to be going to a country where bilateral relations with his own country were so good that he would have ample time to pursue his studies. I asked him in a chat after dinner what subject he planned to major in. "Political science." Book learning after field work. Perhaps international relations courses would have looked usefully to the future not the past.

When I saw the minister-cum-ambassador some months later when he was back on leave, I delicately turned the conversation toward academia. He said nothing about his studies. Perhaps he had found diplomacy a bit more time-consuming than he had expected from seeing people like me in action!

Diplomatic Tables

In some third world countries it is considered polite to accept an invitation and then not show up. Better than refusing the invitation — or, as one

Asian diplomat was alleged to have said, "My wife is expecting to be sick then." This no-show tendency was a bit hard to handle if it was a sit-down dinner. Last-minute table plan changes are irksome. In one capital I would almost invariably slip away from my dinner guests after forty minutes and take up station in the dining room to change the table plan and help the servants juggle the place settings to cover the spaces. I would also have an ear out for some very late arrivals which would require the reshuffle of shuffle. (In Delhi in 1956 I had to work out a table plan for a sit-down multi-table dinner at the Residence for sixty guests. Being then quite green to table plans, I finished these spatial mathematics only minutes before the guests were to arrive. I rushed home to change and missed by inches a charging Delhi bus. Otherwise there would have been a hole in my plan.)

So why not stick to buffets with no plan? There is a joker there. The women still expect or are expected to fill their plates and select a seat first. So as not to be isolated for some minutes they tend to sit together. This may increase the chances of man-to-man work chats at table but there is no guarantee that the most useful combinations will result, and sex segregation offends modern mores. With a table plan you are crimped in your placings by the rules of protocol but there is some flexibility. Once we lost ten out of forty guests. But that was easy. It was a sit-down lunch for the new American ambassador in Zambia. We had laid out four tables of ten guests each. One table was quietly removed and the others gently shuffled. The most considerate dinner guest I ever had was a European diplomat, a bachelor. He arrived punctually although looking very ill. He talked with some local guests for an hour and then, seeing that our table would be over-full (if anything) for once, he made quiet excuses of health and slipped away. He died a month later.

Diplomatic Pumping

In addition to hints, facts, and impressions gained at diplomatic lunches and other gatherings, a regular source of information is, of course, the diplomatic call on a cabinet minister or senior official. In the former case it helps to have an official visitor under your wing if you seek to enter the minister's doorway. An impending conference in common between the countries (e.g., a Commonwealth gathering) can, however, be sufficient to initiate and justify the call. Once I went to call on a senior official and found myself waved instead into the Foreign Minister's presence. We had a useful *tour d'horizon*. Later in my office I received a high-dudgeon phone call from the official I had stood up. I told him about my call on his minister. I had naturally assumed that one had subsumed the other. The official phoned back soon afterwards to apologize for his choler. The minister had in fact had an appointment with the Swedish ambassador. Mistaken identity. I felt complimented. The Swede was big, blonde, and handsome. I assumed that the mistake was in his staff not the minister himself. In any case, he could hardly toss me out once in.

In calls on senior officials, often without instructions, no red-hot and intimate secrets are normally exchanged. Both sides know and observe limits and reserves. But within those constraints of security and sovereignty, legitimate and fruitful exchanges result. I found that this applied even in the case of Western and Eastern delegates in the Vienna arms control talks. Caution governed but permitted respectable exchanges. In the case of diplomatic calls on ministries, the main beneficiary is usually the enquiring diplomat. The senior and well-informed official knows that his duty usually lies in giving more than he receives from the limited embassy reservoirs. Experienced diplomats rarely go into these sessions clutching a list to consult. This would probably inhibit official views. Much preferable is to take a mental list on these fishing expeditions and to run through it rather casually and spontaneously. You may forget a point or two but this is preferable to drying up your source by waving a ham-fisted list. Here again diplomacy is the art of subtlety in conventional contexts.

Diplomatic Tarmacs

In addition to National Day parties, ambassador farewell parties, presidential press conferences, the opening of Parliament, the budget speech, religious and secular ceremonies, etc., ambassadors must do tarmac duty. Whenever a foreign leader of stature arrives the envoys are expected to arrive at the airport well in advance to greet the visitor. You have to turn up or send a substitute or you would be conspicuously absent. How come?

Because the corps is lined up in order of precedence with a nudge or two from a protocol officer.

The following extract from a letter to my daughter from Zambia describes my tarmac stint that day during the brief hot season there.

"After a stifling noon reception for East German national day — ill-cooked meats in the eye of the sun — I had three hours at the airport in a hell-born wind and malevolent yellow sun — waiting for the King of Swaziland who was held up in Mozambique by the kindness of his hosts and, I suspect, by a discussion of how to keep down the flow of Mozambican refugees into Swaziland. Meanwhile at Lusaka airport we had much tra-la and folk dancing and President Kaunda interspersed with two glasses of soda water. Finally the King arrived in the dark which annulled the inspection of the honour guard — but not the welcoming swirl of dancers."

Mandela

The diplomatic welcome scenario was sabotaged by crowded enthusiasm when Nelson Mandela arrived at Lusaka airport soon after his release from detention. The arrangements were for head-of-state treatment. Visiting statesmen including Joe Clark, to salute and praise Mandela, were a novel feature. Mandela was, of course, more important to Zambia, then head-quarters of the ANC and leader of the Front Line States against South Africa, than most presidents. An immense and delighted crowd was matched in zeal by scores of journalists. This is where the elaborate and careful Zambian arrangements collapsed in the diplomatic arena. An invading mob of journalists and other trespassers barging into ambas-sadorial turf filled all the space around and in front of the serried envoy ranks. We were surrounded and cut off. The usual handshake — and per-haps even quick word — from Mandela for each ambassador in turn was impossible because of the exploded logistics. This was in fact the only time that this often tedious bit of international protocol had to be abandoned in my years of lining up on tarmacs. And it was certainly one of those times when the waiting would have been worthwhile, although we envoys did eventually have a group meeting with Mandela.

Diplomatic Publicity

Envoys with aid programs are prone and vulnerable to press photos and stories about aid hand-overs and meetings. I was lukewarm about this. Rubbing it in on a regular basis that the country you are in is a charity case seemed to me uncertain terrain. But CIDA liked to get clippings of such events. Thus I have acquired a stack of press clippings of handing over cheques to finance ministers and signing aid agreements with them, holding babies at crèches we aided, and bestowing sewing machines on Women's Institutes. My good-hearted but iconoclastic daughter, Caroline, turned these photos into several albums of hilarious irreverence by adding comic and sometimes naughty captions and balloons of fictitious and very funny comments. I kept these locked in my office safe!

Diplomatic Drivers

They are thought by some to be a wasteful perquisite of ambassadors. They are not. Ambassadors and official visitors are always on the move, and when they are not, the envoy's wife is, in support of the representational program. She usually has her own car for private purposes. Parking in the centre of capital cities is minimal. The official driver does not sit and pick his teeth when the head-of-post pair do not need him. He often drives other Canadian staff as well as running errands and delivering "by-hands".

In fourteen years as an envoy and two other years in India, where we paid for a personal driver needed for multifarious school runs, we had a total of twelve drivers. Four had to be dismissed, one for increasingly sulky hangovers, one for escalating incompetence, one for a gross and fatal breach of instructions, and one for imminent corruption of youth. The latter reeked of unwholesomeness and told sleazy stories to our fourteen-year-old son. One dismissal in India was expensive. We forgot he had taken our spare wheel and tire to be repaired. We did not know where. We never saw them or him again. Another was a genial fool who capped his silliness by opening the car door from inside just in time to have it sheared off by a passing taxi.

One of our best drivers was an ex-police sergeant in Trinidad, Fraser. His experience and savvy were combined with charm and skill. After he retired, our official car was wrecked in an accident. He immediately drove several miles to the Residence to seek news of our welfare (the radio had implied a wipeout of our family) and perhaps a little out of concern for his old friend the car.

Another driver in another country loved to take us on overnight official tours. He was said to have girlfriends and offspring in every town. An office anecdote about this dry-land sailor was that on one occasion a lithe young woman approached him in the compound. His eyes gleamed as he began to chat her up. The girl cried out, "Daddy, don't you recognize me!"

One of our best drivers was impeccable on the road except just before Christmas when the demon drink struck. The sign was that his usual sparse speech burst into a torrent of slurred chat. He was then grounded but he was far too good to dismiss. And this Christmas curse was much reduced after I overwhelmingly lost my temper on the first occasion. The hallmark of another driver was to cause frequent irritation. But his vast local knowledge, his fractured English, and ludicrous attempts to cull advantage from his errands for us provided a source of humour which our official visitors appreciated long after we had grown tired of it.

The best of the bunch was Abraham Machaya, our driver in Zambia and on frequent trips to Malawi. He was a model of dignity, lucid English, and skilled driving of our balky official car. His reliability was total. He was the conductor of his church choir. This gave him a hobby and second-string vocation ideal for a driver. He spent the unavoidable times of waiting for us in studying and arranging music for his choir. I am sure they benefited. Canada-Zambia relations were advanced at the religious grass roots. We attended two special services of all the congregations of Abraham's church gathered together with massed choirs including his own. They soared in song.

Diplomatic Flags

I used to carry the flag, literally. I did not bother at first but during an early visit to a small Eastern Caribbean state its Premier was distressed to find no Canadian flag on my hired car. I refrained from pointing out that some of his sister states provided flag and holder for the Canadian envoy's use but thereafter I played safe and put them in my suitcase. But some years later in the Western Caribbean I grew sloppy. Our honorary consulate had a flag and magnetic holder in stock in Nassau and elsewhere nobody seemed to worry. I aroused myself, however, before a ministerial visit to Belize and had the national identity kit flown over from Nassau. Alas, what worked well in the stately traffic of Nassau fell off on the swift journey to Belmopan. The magnetic holder lacked sufficient magnetism to counter-act the speedy breezes of Belize. But Canadian grit and moxie was not lacking in this protocol crunch. His Excellency (me) sat in the front seat and as we drove into Belmopan, held the flag and holder onto the car bonnet. We swept thus up to the Parliament building.

Two other occasions are worth a note. One was a sports meet in the Caribbean where Canadians had come down to compete. There was a flag-raising ceremony. I raised the Canadian flag with a flourish and sat down with satisfaction; but, the flag was upside down, to the mischievous delight of my children who were watching on television. Another occasion in the same area was a wreath-laying ceremony deep with solemnity. Each envoy was there and laid his national wreath in rotation. A soldier brought the wreath to the ambassador. It went like clockwork until my turn. The designated soldier handed me the designated wreath clearly wrapped in national colours and insignia. It was somebody else's wreath. Some gremlin had switched wreaths. What to do? Demand your own wreath? Request an enquiry? Pass the wreath around? Disrupt and delay a televised annual tribute to the war dead? So I laid the unknown wreath and told the envoy next in line that he might get the Canadian wreath instead of his own. Sure enough a wreath brave in maple leafs arrived via the next military man. My colleague did the needful. Honour was saved all around.

Conclusions. The small states of the Eastern Caribbean liked to see the Canadian envoy visibly present from time to time. Canadian aid was welcome. Canadian imperialism did not exist. The Canadian presence was benign. So why was our flag sometimes *malplacé*? How many maple trees have you seen in the Caribbean?

Diplomatic Language
Conciseness to save the reader's time in reports and memos is the key rule. There are also certain taboos. When I was junior officer in Ottawa I was told never to use the word "felt" instead of "believed" or "thought." You

only feel with your hands or some other part of the body. And never say "so" when you mean "so that" as a conjunction, a rule I still break. I tried during my career to launch and nourish two useful words of my own. One, in my view, was crying to be born. "Underlap" is surely the very logical and useful opposite of "overlap." I made perhaps some limited progress on this by using the word in occasional reports. I also advocated "deprove" as the sparkling opposite number to "improve." Alas, I seemed to be making no progress in seminating this constructive addition to diplomatic reports. The situation deproved if anything. A loss to the language. Authors are still required to use longer substitutes (e.g., "deteriorate" or "go down hill" or "become worse"). Brevity should be the soul of diplomacy but often is not.

Diplomatic Verse

I carried to Jamaica from Vienna an enjoyable bad habit, doggerel and limericks. I wrote in Vienna a rhyming history of each negotiating round, for Western ears only. Lampoons of the opposing players and tactics would not have amused the Easterners. At a joint East-West farewell lunch for me, however, I read out a paean of poetic praise for the denizens of both camps.

In Jamaica — and then in Zambia — I switched to Christmas limericks for each of my Canadian colleagues. Praising twenty-five colleagues with some shadow at least of veracity and some semblance of rhyme was an amiable strain. I hope it was worth the gain in staff morale, if any. Actually, it must have caused a faint chuckle here and there because the staff responded in kind on our departure. At a farewell party, they gave Nina and me a set of verses extracted from each of our colleagues. This was a rather endearing souvenir accompanied by a cheerful painting of Blue Mountain, an echo of various tramps up it.

Sometimes my verse, I thought, attained to "some poetic strain." This was the case, I hoped, with a verse of farewell to a departing senior colleague, the able and articulate Cliff Garrard, who was married to a lovely blonde called Felicity. So naturally the limerick began with Hamlet's dying words to his friend Horatio urging him to stay alive in the cruel world to tell Hamlet's story. My adaptation began thus: "Absent thee from Felicity awhile, But that's not our Clifford's style," etc., etc. Bad verse in a felicitous cause.

Antigua was the honeymoon site for a friend and lent itself to a limerick:

Thus spake a young chap in Antigua,
"I know just the thing to intrigue her,
I'll give her a punch
Of rum before lunch,
And she'll think that my mouse is a tiga!"

Dry Diplomacy

During a routine medical examination in 1987 I was asked if I had had hepatitis recently. No and never. Two specialists and a scan later I was told that some livers were stronger than others. Mine was in the latter group. I was advised to drop immediately and completely the use of alcohol. I did. I found this sharp change in habit fairly easy to make even though I had been since age eighteen a steady medium-grade drinker with a sometimes hearty increase at parties. Diplomatic life involved lubricants in various measures.

My resolve to undertake my last post in full abstention was aided by cow-ardice. Soon after we got to Lusaka I read by chance an essay which described a patient dying from cirrhosis of the liver in a ward of a public hospital in Paris. The patient's liver was spread across the bed while his small fish mouth gasped dying breaths. Dry diplomacy seemed preferable. To avert boring enquiries about my curious rejection of diplomatic fuel, I let my wine glass be filled. I took two or three almost non-existent sips from it during the meal. Since it remained full, there was no need to draw attention by refusing refills. I joined the official toasts by wetting my lips.

Was dry useful to my work? Yes and no. My head remained clear, "while all about you are losing theirs and blaming it on you" — to adapt Kipling, who was not talking about alcohol. I suppose I sometimes garnered the views of senior locals and of other diplomats with slightly more detailed lucidity than I would otherwise have done. But I probably lost some diplomatic yards by not being able to swing as easily in the genial camaraderie which Africans enjoy.

CHAPTER SEVENTEEN

Retirement

WHEN I RETIRED in September 1990, after thirty-eight years of service, I was one of only four officers who had enjoyed or endured five full postings as ambassador or high commissioner. Ottawa's often turgid pace did not agree with me. Abroad did. None of my five postings as head of mission was in a top post, although Jamaica was certainly a large post with many lively Canadian ties and interests. A subsequent incumbent there had been a deputy minister. I might have ended up nearer the top if I had not preferred to work abroad where the challenges were more challenging. Being boss there was to be a real boss.

I was lucky to get a ripe collection of posts. I once explained to an Irish priest in Zambia, who had noted my wide range of ambassadorships, that I had followed the old saying that it is better to be number one in hell than number two in heaven. I then blanched at this stark mismatch of example and audience. The priest laughed indulgently.

I lunched on my first day of "freedom" with my first boss abroad, Escott Reid. This seemed happily appropriate. Although the presence in the area of old colleagues and friends was an Ottawa magnet and we had a good if decaying house, we did not retire there. We found Ottawa too cold, too full of civil servants and unattractive buildings. And of stodgy memories of past jobs.

Instead we followed a plan hatched in Zambia in our final months. Our eyes had caught with surmise on our Lusaka dining table a Bartlett print table mat. It was dated 1845 and showed red-coated soldiers looking down from an adjoining height onto an attractive limestone town, Kingston, Ontario. Nina was a Queen's graduate and I had enjoyed short visits there in recent years. So we scoured the Kingston area after retirement. We were in luck. After inspecting a welter of houses on islands dependent on ferries and licked by cold lake winds, we found a lovely old stone house in an inland valley with extensive fields and woods attached. It had been restored a few years before. We had only to walk into it. And we did. Caroline suggested we had settled there because the valley, creek, and marsh reminded us of an African game park. Perhaps. Certainly our visits to the African bush convinced us that we could never live in a city again. And we savour the fact that our house was built in 1840, five years before Bartlett portrayed Kingston.

Reece stone house, 1991.

Index